Are you a disillusioned Christian?

Are you experiencing spiritual burnout?

Do you find yourself feeling calloused and cynical toward other Christians?

Are you confused why God would allow good things to happen to bad people . . . or angry that He has not answered your prayers?

Do you wish you could stop feeling this way?

There is hope. You can conquer your disillusionment and rejuvenate your commitment to Christ. Read on . . .

Pro. 3:5,6

The *Disillusioned* Christian

KEN ABRAHAM

Here's Life Publishers

First Printing, July 1991

Published by
HERE'S LIFE PUBLISHERS, INC.
P. O. Box 1576
San Bernardino, CA 92402

Library of Congress Cataloging-in-Publication Data
Abraham, Ken.
    The disillusioned Christian : advice for the burned and the burned out / Ken
Abraham.
        p.   cm.
   ISBN 0-89840-328-6
   1. Christian life—1960- I. Title.
BV4501.2.A22   1991
248.8'6—dc20   91-17435
                               CIP

Scripture quotations are from *The New American Standard Bible,* © The
Lockman Foundation 1960, 1962, 1963, 1968, 1971, 1972, 1975, 1977.

Cover design by Michelle Treiber with David Marty Design

For More Information, Write:
L.I.F.E.—P.O. Box A399, Sydney South 2000, Australia
Campus Crusade for Christ of Canada—Box 300, Vancouver, B.C., V6C 2X3, Canada
Campus Crusade for Christ—Pearl Assurance House, 4 Temple Row, Birmingham, B2 5HG, England
Lay Institute for Evangelism—P.O. Box 8786, Auckland 3, New Zealand
Campus Crusade for Christ—P.O. Box 240, Raffles City Post Office, Singapore 9117
Great Commission Movement of Nigeria—P.O. Box 500, Jos, Plateau State Nigeria, West Africa
Campus Crusade for Christ International—Arrowhead Springs, San Bernardino, CA 92414, U.S.A.

To my brothers,
John and "Tink" Abraham,
who have been just as disillusioned as anyone,
but who still love Jesus and live for Him,
regardless of the costs.
Thanks, guys, for your examples
and encouragement.

Contents

248.8
Abr

1

This Isn't the Trip
I Signed Up For!

*Nobody ever warned you that there would
be times when God seemed a million miles away.*

I was relaxing poolside at a sun-drenched Hawaiian hotel, along with several friends, when I saw Karen coming. She was an attractive woman I guessed to be in her mid-thirties, and she wore a black bathing suit with bright-colored flowers on it. A white hotel towel topped her tousled hair while another large beach towel hung from her waist, hiding her legs from view. An oversized pair of black sunglasses shielded her eyes from the bright sunlight.

As we watched her approach, the look on her face told me: *This woman is not happy.*

"I'm extremely disappointed," she announced to our group without even saying hello. "I wish I would never have come along on this trip."

"Karen, you've got to be kidding!" I objected. "You're in Hawaii, staying at this beautiful hotel with several hundred of your Christian brothers and sisters for a week of spiritual refreshment and physical relaxation. What more could you want?"

"Yeah, well, you guys lied to me!"

"Lied to you? What are you talking about?"

She took off the huge sunglasses, revealing her puffy, swollen eyes.

"That's right," she fired back at me. "You guys promised that this vacation was going to be the trip of a lifetime. You said that I'd have non-stop fun and excitement, that I would meet all sorts of wonderful, new friends, that I'd be refreshed physically, emotionally and spiritually. Satisfaction guaranteed! Well, none of that has happened!"

I stood up and walked over to Karen's side. "Karen, look over there. That's Waikiki Beach. Look at that gorgeous, blue ocean and the soft sand. Feel the warm tradewinds blowing and watch the palm trees swaying in the breeze. (I was beginning to feel like a travel agent!)

"Look, you've got a great group of Christians with whom you can fellowship. Or, if you prefer, there are all sorts of opportunities to share your faith with unbelievers down at the beach. You could go sailing, or try surfing or snorkeling, or just kick back, relax and do some sunbathing. And there are enough stores and boutiques within walking distance so you could shop till you drop! How could you possibly be unhappy?"

"I don't know, but I am!" she retorted. "I'm really disappointed." She replaced her dark glasses and spoke bitterly, "This is *not* the trip I signed up for!"

Not Exactly What We Thought It Would Be

A lot of Christians are feeling like Karen these days, but not about a week-long vacation. They are jaded and jaundiced about their entire journey with Jesus. Many dedicated, well-meaning Christians are disillusioned. For a variety of reasons, they are saying, "Hey, this is not the trip I signed up for!"

Some signed on with Jesus under false pretenses. They were told that the trip would bring a constant effusion of love, joy, peace, excitement and contentment—satisfaction guaranteed. Nobody mentioned that the passengers might encounter danger, frustration and disappointment.

Others were attracted to Jesus by a misguided promise of health, wealth and prosperity. Your body could be healed because it is God's will for all of us to be healthy. Your checkbook could be blessed because God wants you to prosper even as your soul prospers. Your social life will certainly improve because, after all, look at all the wonderful people taking this trip along with you.

Nobody ever warned you that there would be times when God seemed a million miles away. Or you might pray for somebody to be healed and they would die. Where were those financial blessings when you needed them, like when it came time to pay the rent? And what about all those great Christian superstars who have let you down?

Still others are disillusioned because they haven't been able to accomplish what they set out to do. They enlisted in the early days of what we now fondly refer to as "The Jesus Movement." While college students picketed at Kent State, rock'n'roll reigned at Woodstock and radicals resisted the Vietnam draft, many of us saw Christianity as the one true way to change our world. Unfortunately, here we are more than twenty years later, and it still hasn't happened. The world appears every bit as hell-bent now as it did when we sang in the streets of Dallas at Explo '72.

Consequently, many of the Christian baby-boomers feel as though they have already shot their best bullets and so have resigned themselves to expecting nothing more than spiritual boredom and biblical blahs. A major yawn characterizes their lives.

Some of our friends set out to change the world for Christ by giving up everything they owned in the process (houses, cars, relationships and bank accounts), believing they could make a difference. By and large, they didn't. And today, many of these brothers and sisters are on the spiritual sidelines, wondering, sometimes aloud but more often to themselves, "Did I make a mistake? This isn't the trip I signed up for."

One of my best buddies is now a disillusioned Christian. We studied together at Asbury College and Asbury Theological Seminary. When I first met him, I thought Matt was one of the most dedicated, disciplined Christians I had ever encountered. Early each morning, while most of the guys in my dorm (including me!) were trying to steal a few extra minutes of sleep, Matt was already awake, showered and dressed, sitting at his desk or kneeling by his bed, reading his Bible and praying. He was that sort of guy.

Before coming to Asbury, Matt had attended an extremely strict and regimented non-accredited Bible college. He learned well the school's dogmatic approach to biblical interpretation and what it meant to be a "disciplined" Christian: memorizing Scripture, meeting quotas and witnessing to sinners. Matt's creed, inherited from his legalistic mother and reinforced by his reactionary Bible college professors, was simple: "Keep the rules and you will be accepted; break the rules and you're dead."

Throughout his years at college and seminary, Matt kept the rules. Following his graduation, Matt embarked upon his ministry as a missionary. He struggled through language school in a foreign country only to discover, to his dismay, that he could not grasp the many different dialects of the natives to whom he had come to minister.

After more than eight years of preparing to be a missionary, Matt's life on the field was fraught with nothing but failure, fear and unfruitfulness. Worse still, to his horror, Matt suddenly realized he could no longer keep the rules.

At first, he was appalled at his inability to measure up

to the mission board's standards. He worked harder than ever—to no avail. After one defeat followed another, Matt gradually grew indifferent to his failure.

He allowed his spiritual disciplines to lapse. He rarely read his Bible. He prayed even less, except for agonizing, seemingly unanswered cries for God's help. As his attitude degenerated, Matt began to curse and swear. He started to drink. He rebelled against all authority and moral restraint, willfully surrendering to lustful fantasies and eventually allowing latent homosexual tendencies to surface.

When the mission board discovered Matt's spiritual condition, they expelled him and shipped him home. No rehabilitation. No counseling. No loving, caring encouragement. Only more rigid discipline: "You didn't keep the rules; now you're dead."

Matt returned home a spiritual, emotional and physical wreck. He sought help from some former friends and colleagues, but received only further condemnation. His downhill slide accelerated.

Nearly fifteen years later, I unexpectedly bumped into my college buddy. I recognized him immediately. Outwardly, he hadn't changed a bit, but as soon as he opened his mouth, I knew I was talking with a different guy. He belched out a litany of four-letter words and then stood back, as though waiting for me to castigate him.

Instead, I said, "Matt, let's go some place and talk." We did . . . for hours, well into the night and on to the next morning. Matt poured out his story, in fragments at first and then a rushing torrent of discouragement, disillusionment and failure. He readily admitted that he had frequently contemplated committing suicide.

"The only thing that keeps me from blowing my brains out," he said with a pathetic laugh, "is all that hell-fire stuff I learned back in Bible school. I'm sick of living, but I'm too scared to die."

I want to tell you that Matt repented of his sinful disobedience, returned to the mission field and now enjoys a bountiful harvest in the ministry. That's the way it's *supposed* to work, isn't it?

Unfortunately, I can't tell you that because it's not true. As far as I know, Matt is still a disillusioned, bitter, resentful Christian, hanging onto life only because he's afraid to die.

Disillusionment Strikes Us All

Few truly dedicated men or women of God have not experienced the depression and discouragement brought about by spiritual disillusionment.

After being beaten and placed in the torturous stocks for obeying God and speaking the truth, the prophet Jeremiah complained:

> Oh LORD, Thou hast deceived me and I was deceived; Thou hast overcome me and prevailed. I have become a laughingstock all day long; everyone mocks me. . . . for me the word of the Lord has resulted in reproach and derision all day long (Jeremiah 20:7,8).

In commenting upon this passage, eminent preacher and author Charles R. Swindoll wrote:

> Personally, I cannot bring myself to chide Jeremiah. The heavens above him appeared as brass. His Lord's passivity disillusioned him. The silence of God was more than he could take. There are such times, I openly confess, when I, too, wonder why He permits certain things to occur that seemingly defy His character.
>
> At those times I'm tempted to say what the prophet said: "I will not remember Him or speak anymore in His name . . . " (20:9a).
>
> "That's it! I'm tossing in my collar. No more sermons and devotionals for this preacher. Secular job here I come!" But right about the time I start to jump, I experience what Jeremiah admitted:

"Then in my heart it becomes like a burning fire shut up in my bones; and I am weary of holding it in, and I cannot endure it" (20:9*b*).

Directly sent from God is this strong surge of hope, this cleansing fire of confidence, this renewed sense of determination swelling up within me. The disillusionment is quietly replaced with His reassurance as He reminds me of that glorious climax to the hymn I often sing back to Him in full volume: "All is well, all is well!"

Thank God. Recently, I doubted that—like Jeremiah. But not today. Reassurance has returned. Divine perspective has provided a fresh breeze of hope in the pits. I have determined that disillusionment must go.

Now . . . not later.[1]

It is encouraging to me just to know that such a strong Christian leader deals regularly with disillusionment.

Hitting Close to Home

One of my first brushes with spiritual disillusionment came when I was an eighteen-year-old college student sitting on the board of elders at my home church. I had only been a Christian for two years, which may give you a hint regarding the depth of leadership in our church at that time. Nevertheless, the Lord was able to use me in that position as a catalyst for positive change.

When our pastor left for the mission field, the board was faced with the difficult and awesome responsibility of "calling" another man of God to lead the congregation. It was during the interviewing process that my spiritual disillusionment was born.

As the board members talked at length with each potential candidate, I was appalled at the questions they were asking.

"Pastor, does your wife know how to play the piano?"

one elderly woman on the board asked.

"No, Ma'am, she doesn't," the candidate replied courteously.

"Well, would she be willing to learn?" the woman pressed.

"Er, I don't think so," the pastor responded.

Another board member asked, "Do you know how to fix lawnmowers? We have several mowers in the church basement and nobody can get them to work. Think you could handle it?"

The pastor looked at me for some sense of support. I just shook my head and buried my head in my hands.

"That commode downstairs hasn't worked in years. Do you know anything about plumbing, Pastor?"

As the interviews proceeded, I soon realized that the church leaders were not looking for a great Bible expositor, a proven leader or a person with a compassionate pastor's heart. They were looking for a song-leading, piano-playing handyman who could moonlight as a preacher!

And these were the people to whom I was expected to look for spiritual wisdom and counsel?

My initial experience as a church board member was disillusioning, but I fared no better when I began speaking at churches around the country. In the early days of my ministerial career as a traveling preacher, I made a decision to accept speaking engagements on a "free-will offering" basis. To this day I still do the same, which allows me to speak to smaller groups as well as larger congregations.

In one large church where I was the guest speaker, the pastor made an eloquent plea for liberality from the congregation, especially the visitors who had come in for the service.

"I want you to know that *every* penny that comes in through this offering tonight will go to Brother Abraham," the pastor emphatically stated, and then added, "after expenses, of course."

That should have raised my suspicions, but it didn't. I guess I was too naive. I did wonder, *What expenses? I drove here in my own car, paid for my own hotel room and bought my own meals. What is he talking about?*

I had even sent the pastor free promotional materials and posters to put up in his church and around town.

When the evening service was over, the pastor quickly disappeared, even before all the people had exited the building. As I was shaking hands with the last group to leave the sanctuary, the church treasurer came by, shook hands and gave me a sealed envelope.

"Pastor had to go, but he asked me to make sure that you received your honorarium from tonight's offering."

I thanked him kindly and placed the envelope in my briefcase as the treasurer walked away. *Mmm, honorarium?* I thought. *I'm sure the pastor and I had agreed that I would receive whatever amount came in through the offering, whether it was large or small.* By now everyone was gone and the custodian was patiently holding the front door open for me.

I headed for my hotel.

When I got to my room, I took the envelope out of my briefcase and pulled out the check. It was made out to me in the amount of $50. Now, I am grateful for every offering I have ever received, regardless of the amount, but something didn't feel right about this one. *There must be some mistake,* I thought. *Something's not right here.*

The following week my suspicions were confirmed. A friend called who had attended the service in the large church. She was extremely upset.

"Ken, I'm really concerned," she blurted into the phone.

"Why? What's wrong, Debbie?"

"Did you receive my check in the offering when you spoke in our town last week?" she demanded to know.

"Check? What check? The only check I received was a check from the church."

"Well, I'm not looking for your appreciation or anything like that, but I put a check in the plate for $100."

"One hundred dollars!" I exclaimed. "Debbie, thank you very much. That was so nice of you . . . "

She cut me off. "It's not the amount, Ken. My question is, did you get the check?"

"Well, not exactly, I guess. The church gave me a check for $50 . . . "

"Fifty dollars?" she cried. "Ken, I gave you $100 myself! Do you mean to tell me that nobody else in that church gave you a dime? I can't believe that. I saw two fellows in the row where I was sitting put in two twenties. And my mom put in $10; that's $150 right there! And they gave you a check for only fifty?"

"Well, you know, the pastor did say they would give me what was remaining after expenses," I protested, still attempting to give the pastor the benefit of the doubt.

"Expenses! What expenses? Ken, let me tell you why I called about this in the first place. I wrote out a check to you personally and put it in the offering. When I received my cancelled checks from the bank today, I noticed that the signature on the check didn't look anything like yours. I've seen your handwriting before. You signed one of your books for me, remember? Anyhow, I think somebody at that church forged your name on that check and that's illegal."

"Now, take it easy, Debbie. Nobody would do something like that. Not at a church. Surely, they could have asked me to sign my personal checks. I was the last one to leave the building, except for the custodian."

"I'm going to call that pastor and find out what's going on here," Debbie declared.

"No, no. You better let me take care of this. I'll let you know what I find out."

What I found out was that I had been ripped-off by a spiritual leader whom I had respected. The money wasn't the issue; it was the principle. Furthermore, I felt as though the pastor had used me to dupe the people into giving when, in fact, their gifts were diverted to another recipient.

This was the first time I realized that not all the members of God's team were playing straight. Sadly, it would not be the last.

Is there help for the disillusioned Christian? Can dedicated disciples who find themselves running on empty come back to the joy of the Christian life? Better still, can disillusionment be prevented?

These are just some of the questions we're going to explore in this book. It may not be the book you thought it would be. You'll find very few easy answers here. But if you have the courage to honestly face the facts, I believe that the Spirit of Jesus can remove any blinders from your eyes.

I've been down the dry, lonely road of disillusionment. I can relate to your struggle. It's not a fun trip. It's not the trip you signed up for. But from one disillusioned Christian to another, let me tell you, there is hope. Real hope. Come on and see.

2

Welcome to Your
Spiritual Mid-Life Crisis

*Despite your most valiant efforts, you are discovering
that your spiritual life just isn't working.*

Maybe it was my age. Or perhaps it was the discovery
of that first grey hair upon my head. Whatever the
reason, I have been mulling over a mental list of common
symptoms that might indicate a person is experiencing a
mid-life crisis. Here are a few signs I have noticed:

- Boredom and exhaustion; or sometimes the opposite: a frantic running to and fro, expending
  enormous amounts of energy, often accompanied
  by the feeling that you are accomplishing extremely
  little of any real significance

- Self-questioning; deep-seated self-doubts

- Daydreaming

- Irritability or unexpected anger

- Compulsions (alcohol, drugs, cigarettes or food)

- Greatly decreased sexual desire; or the opposite
  extreme: a surprising temptation to enter into an
  affair (that innocuous sounding euphemism for what

the Bible condemns as adultery or fornication)

- An urgent desire for *change*; usually, this is a radical, unanticipated change, such as suddenly seeking a new job, moving to another city or to another part of the country

- Greatly decreased or increased ambition; this some-times shows up as indifference or ambivalence toward your work, or a maddening "workaholism" where you can never do enough to satisfy yourself

In addition, the person who is experiencing a mid-life crisis is easily distracted, feels unchallenged and un-motivated, and is frequently depressed, discouraged and doubtful about his or her ability to cope. He or she begins to question basic values and long-held assumptions about the priorities established in one's life, perhaps even ques-tioning the purpose for life itself.

Granted, many of the characteristics on the above list could also be symptoms of adolescence, old age or eating too many hot peppers at a Mexican restaurant. Neverthe-less, when several of the traits begin showing up in your life concomitantly, you can no longer shrug them off as mere "psycho-babble." Something is wrong!

In his highly recommended book, *Men in Mid-Life Crisis*, pastor and counselor Jim Conway describes his own disillusionment:

> My depression had grown all through the spring, summer and fall. By October it reached giant propor-tions. I would often stare out the window or simply sit in a chair, gazing into space . . . I had literally come to the bottom of me. I was ready to chuck everything. Repeatedly, I had fantasies of getting on a sailboat and sailing off to some unknown destination where no one knew me and where I carried no responsibility for anyone in my church or my family. . . .

On a cold, wintry night, I went for a long walk and made some decisions. I would resign as pastor of the church, write a letter to Fuller Seminary to tell them I was dropping my doctoral program, and write to my publishers to tell them I no longer would be writing. I would also legally turn everything over to Sally, take only our 1968 Cutlass, and start driving south. For me, it was all over. I had had it with people, with responsibility, with society, even with God, who had been such a close friend all of my adult life. He seemed now to be distant and remote, uninterested in the agony through which I was going. . . .

I felt like the proverbial Humpty Dumpty who had just come crashing off the wall, and all the king's horses and all the king's men couldn't possibly put my life back together.[1]

Quite possibly, you are experiencing something similar in your spiritual life. Despite your most valiant efforts, you are repeatedly discovering that your spiritual life just isn't working. Something is wrong! But what? Perhaps, you are in the midst of what I call a "Spiritual Mid-Life Crisis."

What Is a "Spiritual Mid-Life Crisis"?

Understand, I am not questioning your salvation. If you have committed your life to Jesus Christ and trusted Him as your Savior, you are a Christian. On the other hand, if you don't have a relationship with Jesus, you are not disillusioned; you are *lost* and need to be saved.

Assuming, however, that you began well, that you established a *bonafide* relationship with Christ and you started out with a great deal of energy and enthusiasm, allow me to guess what may have happened to bring you to your present condition.

Someone squelched your zeal, right? I thought so. When you first came to Jesus, you were so excited about your faith. You wanted the whole world to know. Then you encountered some sanctimonious "saint" who smiled condescendingly as he snidely sneered, "Calm down . . . calm down! Wait and see. Soon your joy will disappear and you will be just like the rest of us."

God forbid! My brother has a poster framed and prominently displayed in his office. It says simply: "Lord, preserve us from sour-pussed saints." Sometimes the worst thing that can happen to a new Christian is to meet an "old" one, one who has been on the way so long that he has lost the joy of the Lord's salvation.

The Christian life is not supposed to work that way. Yet if you are like most other believers, you have probably met more than your share of "sour-pussed saints" by now. They drain your energy; they impede your spiritual passion and progress; they are often major contributors toward your disillusionment; and they hasten the approach of your spiritual mid-life crisis.

Perhaps you've been burned by other believers, done dirty by the disciples, fried by friends in the fellowship. You know how it goes: You were spiritually battered, beaten and bruised, looking up from the bottom, when you finally decided to take a chance. You opened up and reached out to a Christian brother or sister for help. To your surprise, rather than receiving a helping hand, you received the "right foot of fellowship" (a swift kick to the rear) followed by a knife in the back. Those from whom you logically expected spiritual help became yet another burden.

My friend Gary S. Paxton, a Grammy-award-winning record producer, musical artist and songwriter, penned a composition titled, "Only Christians Kill Their Wounded." Sad . . . but true. Gary has a slogan he keeps posted in his recording studio, a studio primarily popularized and frequented by Christian recording artists and recording company personnel. It reads:

I've been poked, pulled, punched, beaten up,

kicked, lied to, cheated, ripped-off, and robbed. The only reason I hang around this place is to see what's gonna happen next.

Do you know that feeling? Just beneath the surface festers a cynical mistrust of anything or anybody that uses the term "Christian" as an adjective. For example: Christian businessmen (so many in this category have compromised and squandered away their ethical principles that the term is almost considered an oxymoron), Christian artist, Christian ministry.

It's not that you don't *believe* anymore; you do! But you have become disillusioned, discouraged and disheartened. Probably a number of other dirty "D" words describe your life: distressed, depressed, disgusted, distant, dismayed . . . you get the idea.

Furthermore, it's not that your faith in God has failed; you're just not as confident about committing to *God's people* anymore. You still trust Christ, but you wouldn't trust most *Christians* any further than you could throw them! Your dreams have been dashed. Your expectations and your experience have proven to be poles apart.

Your Personal Power Shortage

Sometimes a person's spiritual mid-life crisis cannot be connected to any external cause. Sometimes it is linked solely to his or her inability to live the Christian life the way the Bible explains. A power shortage exists within the person's heart.

As you compare your experience to the biblical record, a perplexing array of questions about your life haunts your mind:

- Can't God do more than *this* in and through my life?

- Is this the kind of life that Jesus had in mind when

He died that I might live?

- Did He allow the soldiers to crucify Him—putting nails in His hands and feet, forcing a crown of thorns upon His head, piercing His side with a sword and receiving the jealous jeers of ancient Jerusalem—so I might continue to make a mockery of His name?

- Does God really intend for me to live at such a low level of spiritual maturity, a life of perpetual defeat, constant struggle and seemingly endless weariness?

- Why do I find myself unable to resist temptation, repeatedly returning to the same sins that I know Jesus died to deliver me *from?*

- The Bible says that Jesus came to break the power of sin and destroy the works of the devil. Why, then, do I have such little power over sin and the devil's attempts to thwart God's work in my life?

Sound familiar? If you've been on that road for long, you probably don't need me to inform you that you're traveling a downhill path.

When you first came to know Jesus, it all seemed so simple. Remember how bold you were, how absolutely assured of spiritual victory? You confidently declared the message of Christ to anyone who would listen, rarely worrying about your reputation or your welfare. You almost naively plunged into dangerous waters, believing completely that you were "more than a conqueror through Him who loved you." With Jesus as your divine commander, you hardly dared dream of anything but spiritual success.

Unfortunately, your fearlessness quickly began to fade after a few disastrous defeats. Your victories came fewer and farther apart while your "won-loss" ledger leaned heavily in the wrong direction.

Such spiritual defeat often triggers doubt and unbelief.

Now when you pray (*if* you pray), you honestly don't anticipate hearing an answer from God. Certainly you seek the Lord's assistance when you are sick, but you have long since given up believing that God would actually heal your body. You quit looking for answered prayers of any kind a long time ago.

You still read the Bible occasionally. Maybe you have even acquired some measure of knowledge of its principles. Yet you have been able to put few of its precious promises into practice. You ponder, *Surely, the promises of God must work for somebody*, somewhere, but why don't they work in my life?

Listening to inspiring sermons from your pastor only exacerbates the problem. After all, contemplating the incredible courage of "Daniel in the Lion's Den" does little to pull you out of your own pits. And hearing how young David stood up to giant Goliath only causes you to feel more depressed when you think of your own inability to prevail over the puny obstacles in your path.

One anonymous insightful observer of Christians put it this way:

> You seem to have a religion that makes you miserable. You are like the man with a headache. He doesn't want to get rid of his head, but it sure hurts him to keep it![2]

Your spiritual well is dry. Your soul is starving for something besides the parched morsels you have been feeding it. You feel your candle is flickering, on the verge of going out altogether. Despite all you know about God, Jesus, the Bible, the church and Christianity, it all seems to be talk. Nice words. Challenging words. Motivating words. But words without life. Mere words.

If you were forced to tell the truth, you'd have to admit that you really don't know Jesus very well, and at times, you wonder if He, like Santa Claus or the Easter Bunny, is not merely another fictitious fairy-tale type character who doesn't really exist. You have come to the conclusion that the Christian life is a cosmic joke and not a joyful, contented lifestyle after all.

Am I describing you? Such is the despair of a spiritual mid-life crisis. Not a pretty picture, is it?

Unlike a chronologically related, psychological mid-life crisis, a spiritual mid-life crisis is not confined to adults in their middle ages. Young men and women in their early twenties or thirties are equally susceptible, as are saints in their sixties or seventies. Even more disconcerting, it is possible to have multiple spiritual mid-life crises re-occurring throughout your lifetime.

Is There Any Hope?

In a word, *yes*. But before we get to that, it is imperative that you understand this: You are not alone! You are not the first person to experience such disillusionment. Sadly, you will probably not be the last. But you are determined to deal with it. The fact that you are reading this book is an indication of that. Many deeply devoted Christians are struggling with the same questions you are— though they may be too stubborn to admit it.

God must have foreseen disillusionment among His followers. That's why He gives us a much needed word of encouragement through the prophet Isaiah:

> Though youths grow weary and tired,
> And vigorous young men stumble badly,
> Yet those who wait for the LORD
> Will gain new strength;
> They will mount up with wings like eagles,
> They will run and not get tired,
> They will walk and not become weary
>   (Isaiah 40:30,31).

Your heavenly Father is a realist. He doesn't say that you will never run out of your own energy. Nor does He deny your capability of falling from devastatingly high places. In fact, the language that Isaiah uses to convey this message has athletic and military overtones. He is implying that even those who are in tip-top condition, skillfully trained and prepared for battle can fail woefully if they depend upon their own energies. Most Christians are only too familiar with this kind of failure.

The secret of success comes in the second part of the passage: "Yet those who wait for the LORD . . . " *they* will find renewed strength; *they* are the ones who "will mount up with wings like eagles." Furthermore, the Word clearly states that it is *possible* to run the race without running out of resources.

But how? How can this be done? What is this strange, superhuman power that comes only from waiting on the Lord? How can we find it, and how can we maintain this secret supply? That's what we will discover in the pages ahead. But first we must examine some of the reasons Christians become disillusioned.

When Your Best Isn't Good Enough

Ironically, the most dedicated Christian is the leading candidate for spiritual dryness.

Don and Michelle were the modern-day picture of Christian devotion. Raised in Italian-Catholic families, they both brought to their marriage a strong commitment to the family and to the church. Nobody doubted their sincere dedication to the Lord. If there was ever a question about Don and Michelle, it was: "How do they do it all?"

Don coached the Little League team; Michelle led the local Girl Scout troop. He was on the church board and taught the adult Sunday school class; she coordinated the ladies' luncheons and taught the young marrieds class. Together they helped direct the church youth group and both sang in the choir. The doors of the church were rarely open without Don or Michelle or both of them in attendance.

They did all the things that are supposed to bring spiritual happiness. They prayed regularly, both publicly and privately. They tithed their income, giving at least a tenth of their resources to the Lord's work. Consciously or unconsciously, they tithed their time and talents. They told others about Jesus whenever an opportunity arose. They fasted frequently, going without food for a period of time in order to focus more fully upon the Lord. They volunteered to help any time a need existed within the church.

In the late '80s and early '90s, they protested against abortion, marching in public picket lines in front of the State Capitol building as well as participating in nonviolent protests at abortion clinics. They voted in every election and took part in other civic events as well. They attended all of their children's school functions and usually found time to drop in at most parent-teacher organization meetings.

"Model Christians." That's what everyone called them.

Then one day, their spiritual Camelot began to crumble. Denise, their seventeen-year-old daughter, became pregnant. Admirably, Don and Michelle rallied around their daughter, as did the church family, lovingly supporting Denise all through her pregnancy and helping her place the child with a Christian adoption agency. Neither the parents nor the daughter received a single word of condemnation from their church family concerning the premarital pregnancy.

Still, Don and Michelle could not shake their sense of embarrassment. They continued their involvement in church and community activities, but their joy disappeared. Instead, they tortured themselves with questions such as: "Where did we go wrong?" and "How could we have missed Denise's need for love and affection?"

Several months after the birth of the baby, just as they were beginning to see some daylight, Don received a phone call from the police. Their son, Donny Jr., had been picked up and charged with possession of cocaine. That same year, at the Thanksgiving dinner table, Don and Michelle's eldest daughter, Carrie, declared that she had decided to get a divorce from her husband of ten years.

In a matter of months, it seemed that the couple's entire world had collapsed. In desperation, they came to see me. As Don finished telling me their story, he leaned forward in his chair, placing his elbows on his knees and his face in his hands. His voice cracked as he said softly but intensely, "It's not supposed to happen this way. We've been good Christians. We've given everything to God we had to give."

His voice grew louder, "Why didn't God do something to prevent these things? How could our kids have turned out so wrong? What are we supposed to do now, Ken? What do you do when your best isn't good enough?"

What indeed?

As I talked further with the Don and Michelle, I realized that their image as the Model Christian Couple was a facade—a sincere effort to put on their best face, but a fragile mask nonetheless. They had merely been maintaining the appearance of having it all together. In actuality, they were both basket cases on the edge of breakdown.

Don and Michelle's experience illustrates several major causes of spiritual disillusionment. Most significantly, even before their children's problems surfaced, Don and Michelle had been "running on empty" physically, emotionally and spiritually. They were going, going, gone for God, constantly going somewhere, doing something in His name.

In the process, however, they allowed their personal spiritual reservoirs to run dangerously low. Either they didn't realize their condition was fragile, or, if they did, they refused to rectify it. They had entered one of the most dangerous, yet often overlooked, breeding grounds for disillusioned Christians: spiritual dehydration.

Spiritual Dehydration

Even dedicated disciples of Jesus sometimes discover they feel drained out and dried up spiritually. Pastors and other ministry workers often feel this way on Monday mornings, especially if the previous week has been a whirlwind of spiritual activity, culminating in a triumphant celebration of the Lord's Day. After a busy week, I'll frequently say to my wife Angela, "I feel as though somebody unscrewed my feet and drained every ounce of energy out of me!"

Ministry workers aren't the only ones to experience the dragging effects of spiritual dehydration. Anyone who works with the public on a regular basis knows this feeling. Office workers, waiters, teachers, check-out clerks, healthcare workers and a host of other public service workers are equally susceptible to spiritual burnout.

Others who live or work in an extremely stressful environment inevitably find their personal resources running dry. Parents of young children and parents of teenagers often discover their spiritual supplies depleted.

Ironically, the most dedicated Christian is the leading candidate for spiritual dryness. Why? Because it is easy to get so busy doing "God's work" that you have little or no time left to enjoy God's presence.

Don and Michelle made this mistake. They thought doing good deeds for the Lord and maintaining a busy schedule dominated by spiritual activities would sustain their fellowship with Christ. It seemed a logical conclusion to them, and perhaps it makes sense to you as well. But even admirable works are no substitute for fellowship with the Savior.

We've all been warned about this subtle temptation; few of us take it seriously . . . until it's too late. We think that as long as we are busy for God, we are nurturing our relationship with Him. That is not necessarily so. If left unattended, your spiritual life soon becomes as dry as a Saudi Arabian desert.

You Can't Give What You Don't Have

Spiritual dehydration can come not only from constantly giving out, but also from a failure to adequately replenish your spiritual resources.

Frequently, it is my privilege to speak to pastors and Christian musicians. The issue about which I caution them most emphatically is spiritual dehydration. "You can't give out what you haven't taken in," I tell them. "You think that your relationship with Jesus is proportional to your ministry for Him. It is exactly opposite. Your ministry will come *out* of your relationship with Him. Otherwise, it all becomes a show and a sham."

For most of my life I lived in western Pennsylvania near Pittsburgh, a city most people associate with steel, coal and smoke stacks spewing filth into the air. Not too many years ago that was an accurate description of the town, but no longer. Today the Pittsburgh skyline is one of the prettiest in America. Coming through the Fort Pitt tunnel, one of several mile-long tubes that delivers traffic to the downtown area, I watch as the city explodes into a panoramic vista right before my eyes. Regardless of how many times I've seen it, it is still an awe-inspiring sight.

One day as I approached the tunnels at rush hour, I encountered a huge traffic jam. Cars and trucks stood in line for miles, waiting to get through the tubes. As traffic inched down a hill toward the tunnels, more vehicles joined the chain, further clogging the already overloaded highway system. Tempers flared and radiators overheated, complicating the situation further. What should have been a twenty minute drive from the airport to the city took me nearly two hours.

The evening newscasters that night revealed the unlikely cause of the delay. A car had run out of gas in the middle of the tunnel and the owner and his family sat in the auto petrified by fear (not to mention the abusive remarks from other drivers as they passed by). Afraid to get out of the car and go for help, they remained stymied and stalled in the center of the fast lane.

Not only had the driver jeopardized himself, but he also had endangered his entire family and created a potential disaster for hundreds of other people. Thankfully, no major catastrophe occurred, but the man certainly clogged up the system and inconvenienced a massive number of men, women and children.

The same thing happens when you run dry spiritually. You may be the one to run out of gas, but the ramifications of your emptiness impact everyone around you. A pastor's dryness portends death to his congregation; a father's empty tank will take its toll on his family members; a boss whose spiritual reservoir is dry will make a poor spiritual impression upon his or her employees. Dozens, sometimes hundreds, possibly even thousands, of other people are negatively affected whenever *one* Christian allows himself or herself to run out of gas spiritually. A classic example of this can be seen in the life of King David.

A Hero Takes a Fall

After King Saul had been killed on the battlefield, David, the anointed successor, traveled to Hebron of Judah according to the Lord's instructions. There David established his power base and became King of Judah, the smaller of the two parts of divided Israel. Later, after winning a civil war, David consolidated his power and became king over both Judah and Israel. The first ten chapters of 2 Samuel are, for the most part, chronicles of David's mighty exploits on the battlefield. Then comes chapter eleven, one of the most infamous accounts in Scripture—the tragic story of David and Bathsheba.

You are probably familiar with the details: how David

stayed back in Jerusalem while his armies went out to fight;
how he was walking around the roof of his home one night
and spied beautiful Bathsheba bathing below; how he sent
his messengers to bring Bathsheba to him; how he had sex
with her, even though both were married; how, when
Bathsheba became pregnant, David attempted to dupe her
husband, Uriah, by bringing him home from the battlefront
in order to sleep with his wife.

When Uriah nobly refused David's offer to return
home to his wife, David sent him back to the front. With
orders to General Joab to put him in the thick of the fighting,
David virtually authorized Uriah's murder. Uriah died while
in battle and, following a proper period of feigned mourning, David took Bathsheba to be his wife (he had several
wives already).

As you read the account, you almost want to cry out,
"David! Mighty man of God! Leader of God's people. How
could you allow this to happen?"

I believe at least part of the answer lies in David's
spiritual dehydration. He had been running and fighting
since he was a teenager. When he finally became the leader
of the land, his schedule and responsibilities did not lessen.
They intensified. More battles ensued. Enemies came out
of the woodwork. The enemy of your soul does not roll over
and play dead just because you take some territory for God.
You can count on a counterattack.

By the time of David's adulterous liaison with Bathsheba, he was tired physically and empty spiritually. Possibly
he had not taken time to replenish his own spiritual reserves
before going out to battle again. He was so busy fighting
battles *for* God, he had failed to take time *with* God. Sound
familiar?

Consequently, as David peered into the night from
atop his roof, he possessed little spiritual stamina. He had
little interest in the things of God, and he was wide open to

every temptation that the devil could throw at him. Satan knew exactly where to hit him . . . especially since things hadn't been going well between David and his wife, Michal (Saul's daughter). David was sitting in the tunnel, out of gas.

This sin was not a "moment of weakness" on David's part, as has often been preached. David made a series of deliberate decisions and foolish, sinful choices. As a result, he suffered horrible shame, disrepute and tragedy in his own life, and he destroyed many other lives as well. When a man or woman of God runs out of gas in the middle of the road, other people are liable to get hurt, and they usually do.

It was more than a year before David admitted his moral failure and sin. Confession came only after Nathan the prophet confronted the king face to face. That must have been an awful moment in David's life as he was forced to acknowledge his sin. No doubt, he must have wondered a million times, *How could this have happened? Why was I ever so foolish? How could I have gotten into this mess? Why didn't I pay attention to the warning signs? Why didn't I refuel? How could I have allowed myself to get so empty? After years of intimacy with God, and dependency upon His presence, how could I have been so powerless against temptation?*

David probably asked himself such questions for the remainder of his life. Even though forgiveness and restoration are possible, sin leaves indelible marks.

We need not dwell upon David's sin. Only note that part of David's problem may well have been spiritual dehydration which often leads to sin which always ends in disaster. And spiritual disillusionment usually develops somewhere along the way. Not all spiritually dehydrated individuals become disillusioned Christians, but many do.

Vulnerable Victims

Two groups are highly susceptible to spiritual dehydration. The first, as I have already mentioned, are "the hard workers" in the kingdom. We often hear that 80 percent of the work of any church is done by only 20 percent of the people who attend regularly. Obviously, this is an inevitable combination for spiritual burnout. Willing-hearted brothers and sisters can only bear more than their share of the burden for a limited time before they collapse.

Surprisingly, a second group that is highly susceptible to spiritual dehydration is that group we often think of as the "beautiful people." Individuals with a great deal of natural ability—physically attractive people, highly intelligent individuals, fine athletes or successful business men and women—are prone toward spiritual dehydration, as are highly creative individuals—musicians, artists and skilled craftsmen.

Why are these types so vulnerable to this condition? Because they are easily tempted to mistake the applause, approval or admiration of the crowd for the blessing of God.

Sometimes you can see this at professional Christian concerts. A sincere singer may perform a song a certain way and the Spirit of God falls powerfully upon the place. The next night, that same singer may be in another town, several hundred miles away, singing the song again. How tempting it becomes to rely upon the tried and true and think, *Hey, that worked last night; I'll bet it will work again tonight.*

Is that wrong? Not necessarily. But if that singer does not seek to replenish his or her own spiritual well, the song and the patter become nothing more than rote performance, a routine designed to manipulate an audience.

Preachers can succumb to the same snare. As a traveling preacher, it is relatively simple for me to finely hone several messages and keep traveling further distances to deliver them. Who needs to seek God's will? Why waste time praying? That message worked in the last town. Surely, it will elicit the same response tonight.

And it might! But that is no evidence of the anointing of God's Holy Spirit. If I am to be truly effective as a mobile minister, I must seek the Lord's mind for every message I present. I often pray as I prepare for each message, "Lord, what do You want to say through me to this group of people at this particular point in history?" He may, in fact, lead me to a message that I have used many times previously, but if so, that message will have a freshness to me as though it were the first time I presented it.

Time to Check the Gauges

In most automobiles, a variety of gauges, gadgets and gizmos begin to flash red whenever a problem exists, warning that a malfunction is impending if the vehicle is not serviced immediately. Similarly, "red indicators" will warn you of spiritual dehydration. In *Renewing Your Spiritual Passion,* author Gordon MacDonald describes this dried-out condition:

> It is action without heart, oratory without power, doctrine without love. People who are dried out within can often be, for a while, the hardest workers. But they can also become the harshest critics and the most negative teammates.[1]

Let's take a closer look at the red indicators mentioned in that description.

1. A sure sign of spiritual dehydration is *lots of action but improper motivation.* Don and Michelle fell into this trap. Their overextended schedule thinly hid the truth: Their hearts had grown cold. In their case, their intentions were good, but quite often the attitude of the spiritually dehydrated person becomes calloused and critical. And he or she attempts to compensate by getting "busier for God."

2. Another red warning light should go off when you

hear yourself *using spiritual sounding words, but sense little real spiritual power in your life.* Let's face it: Almost anybody can sound spiritual if they just learn the language. Some Christians seem to practically *speak* in Scripture: "Yea, verily, the sun surely doth shineth today!"

The Seven Sons of Sceva, a Jewish chief priest, had heard Paul casting out evil spirits in the name of Jesus. Thinking that the power came by merely repeating the name, they attempted to cast evil spirits out of a demon-possessed man. But the boys had no spiritual power, "and the man in whom was the evil spirit, leaped on them and subdued all of them and overpowered them, so that they fled out of that house naked and wounded" (Acts 19:12-16).

Spiritual words without spiritual power can be dangerous! Are your words empty, hollow chatter, or have you tapped into the genuine, overcoming power of God's Holy Spirit? To have a clean heart and to be filled with Christ's personality and power, you must spend time in His presence. Otherwise, your words will be powerless.

3. Spiritually dehydrated people tend to *dispense large doses of doctrine with very little love.* They know the rules! They just don't keep them. They may talk a lot about the Lord, but their lives are devoid of joy. They have little love and even less compassion.

If you seek help from a spiritually dehydrated person, he or she quite possibly will look down their nose at you as if to say, "Well, my, my! Aren't we the spiritual weakling? *I* conquered that area years ago. Do you mean to tell me that you are still struggling with *that*?" Or they might smile condescendingly as they sniff, "Well, you just need to pray a little more" or "You know, God causes all things to work together for good." Lots of doctrine, very little love.

4. According to Gordon MacDonald, spiritually dehydrated individuals may be *the ministry's hardest workers, but also some of the harshest critics.* Basically,

burned out believers are no fun to be around for any length of time. They are usually negative-minded, critical people, always looking on the down side of things. You may say, "Isn't the sun shining beautifully today?" and they are likely to respond, "Yes, but somewhere it's raining."

They have an unusually strong sense of self-doubt which causes them to criticize others and themselves. Nothing is ever quite good enough. If you compliment them on an achievement, they will immediately begin lamenting how they could have done better.

Spiritually dehydrated individuals do not like themselves. They know that they are not living the Christian life the way it is meant to be lived. Therefore, they harbor an inner anger at themselves and a mistrust of anyone who claims to "have it together" with the Lord. Despite these negative attitudes, spiritually dehydrated individuals honestly cannot comprehend why other people are not clamoring to be their friends.

5. Another indicator of possible spiritual dehydration is *a person suddenly deciding to quit doing the very things he or she loves to do the most.* They are convinced that their time of usefulness is over and they feel powerless to proceed any further. Future efforts would be futile. They are "washed up," over the hill, unable or unwilling to perform any more. Barbara Mandrell experienced something similar to this following a tragic auto accident.

Barbara is a popular entertainer whose accomplishments in country music are legendary: the Country Music Association has honored her with some of its most prestigious awards, including Entertainer of the Year and Female Vocalist of the Year. She has hosted her own network television program and has a personal museum in the heart of Nashville's Music Row. The list of her achievements is long. She also has a strong faith in Jesus Christ.

Nevertheless, when Barbara suffered severe injuries in

a head-on auto collision, she lost the will to perform, the will to pray and almost the will to live. Several months passed and Barbara's body remained racked with pain.

Some of her friends and family members believed that if Barbara could envision performing again, it might be therapy for her and improve her chances for a full recovery. When they suggested the idea to Barbara, the performer repeatedly rejected their encouragement. In her book, *Get to the Heart,* she admits: "My response was, 'Never.' I no longer felt the need to entertain people. That part of my life was over."

Barbara was adamant in her refusals. She writes:

> One time we were having the same old discussion, and they were trying to prod me into trying one performance.
>
> "No!" I shouted. "I am not going back. I am going to stay in my room until I feel better." [2]

Have you ever felt that you would prefer to run away and hide rather than risk future failure or hurt again? Perhaps you have said to yourself, "It's over. There is no use in going any further." In your marriage, on the job or in the ministry God has given to you, there probably have been times when you were ready to throw in the towel. You are not alone.

If you think such thoughts and emotions are reserved for "spiritual sissies," you may be shocked to learn that none other than the founder of the Salvation Army, William Booth, felt the same way. Booth was not what one would call a "wimpy" Christian. In fact, his biographer, Richard Collier, titled Booth's life story, *The General Next to God.*

Booth was a giant of a man in every sense. A large, powerful man, he was totally dedicated to saving souls and serving the Lord through the Salvation Army. He was thoroughly saved and filled with the Holy Spirit.

Despite his physical and spiritual power, Booth felt bereft of both at times. Once, when Booth was on the road for the Lord, lonely and exhausted from his extensive travels and tired of trying to make ends meet financially, he was ready to quit the ministry. The General was ready to go "AWOL," Absent Without Leave. In despair, he wrote to his wife Catherine:

> I wonder whether I could not get something to do in London of some kind, some secretaryship or something respectable that would keep us going. I know how difficult things are to obtain without friends or influence, as I am fixed. But we must hope against hope, I suppose.[3]

Did you catch the thrust of the General's thought? He was saying, "Kate, I wonder if I could find a *real* job someplace?"

As a pastor, author and speaker, I have frequently echoed Booth's sentiments: "I wonder if I could get a job selling used cars? I already own some loud sports jackets." Or, "I hear that Amway is looking for a few good men. I wonder if I could do that?" Or, "McDonalds is hiring. I know how to flip burgers."

The Source of Life for the Spiritually Dehydrated

All of us have been tempted to throw in the towel. Many times, the source of those feelings can be traced back to spiritual dehydration. Rather than tossing towels, turn back to the promise of God:

> Those who wait for the LORD will gain new strength (Isaiah 40:30).

Remind yourself that you are trusting in God's power rather than your own resources. His power is awesome. It is power to create *ex nihilo*, "out of nothing." Isn't that good news? He has power to create beauty, life and, yes, He can even create spiritual energy where the supply has dwindled or where it has been exhausted or where it was previously nonexistent!

Remind yourself of God's great power and willingness to provide. One of His names recorded in the Old Testament is *Jehovah Jireh,* "the God who provides." He is able to provide for you.

Throughout Isaiah 40, God's powerful presence is emphasized. He did not merely crank up the universe, then go off to play golf in some other galaxy. He is not a spectator. He is not like the false gods people tend to worship. He is not an idol of wood or stone.

On the contrary, He is *personally* involved in your world, and He is intimately aware and concerned about the day-to-day details of your life. He is vitally involved in the everyday affairs of the world. Allow this passage of Scripture to remind you that although strong men and women may become drained out or dried up, your great God never does! He is never too tired or too busy to listen and to commune with you. He will hear; He will help. Furthermore, His strength is your source of strength.

When you feel spiritually dehydrated, don't allow foolish pride to cause you to miss Him. Call out His name. Wait upon the Lord. Allow Him enough time to revive and refresh you. Listen for His voice and His promise is that He will renew your strength. That's a promise you can count on, even when your best efforts are not good enough or your most idealistic dreams have gone down the drain.

Ouch! Dashed dreams can sure be a cause for disillusionment among Christians. I'll bet you've had some of those, huh? Me, too. Let's look at a few.

--------------- 4 ---------------

Dashed
Dreams

*Can anyone really pick up the pieces of a shattered
dream and put them back together?*

In 1989, my family and I moved to Nashville, Tennessee.
Nashville is a fun city, a sprawling metroplex with a
small-town attitude. It is known as a bustling railroad center
and as an educational enclave with numerous colleges and
universities. It is home for a plethora of printing and
publishing companies, including several major Christian
book and music publishers. Oh, yes—it is also the state
capital.

Undoubtedly, though, Nashville is best known as
"Music City," the home of the Grand Old Opry and the
headquarters for the Country Music Association and the
Gospel Music Association. Thousands of potential artists
come to town every year with briefcases filled with songs,
hearts filled with dreams and eyes filled with stars. A few of
them make it big. Most end up waiting tables at local
restaurants. Many become disillusioned Christians.

More than twenty years ago, I traveled that same path.
My brothers and I had established a family-oriented evan-

gelistic ministry. We sang gospel songs and preached gospel messages. God honored His Word and many people trusted Jesus Christ as a result of our unprofessional but purely motivated presentations.

All the group members held down full-time jobs or attended high school or college, so at first, our efforts were limited to weekend trips. As the group became more popular locally and regionally, we received invitations to minister in a much broader area. Soon, we were traveling state to state, sharing the gospel and dreaming of an ever-expanding ministry.

People began to tell us that we ought to get into "full-time Christian service." In our evangelistic zeal, we did not realize that *every* Christian is called to full-time service; the only question is where God wants you to serve. One wise wag attempted to guide our decision by advising, "Don't go full-time until you can't afford not to," by which he meant, "Don't quit your secular jobs until you have so many ministry dates scheduled that you can't keep up with them all."

Before long, we believed we had arrived at that crossroads. My brother resigned his secure position with a leading company in our area, I dropped out of seminary, we bought a bus and "hit the road for Jesus." Along the way, we recorded several albums of gospel music, ministered in hundreds of little churches around the countryside and saw literally thousands of people find Jesus Christ.

Somebody suggested that in light of our success, we should go to Nashville to sing and record because that's where all the "big" groups sang. If we were ever going to make it in the music ministry, we had to be where it was happening.

Quite frankly, it never happened for us. "The big break" we dreamed about never materialized. It was always right around the corner, one step away, one more meeting, one more record deal, one more humiliating interview with an entry-level employee of a record company, only to be told, "I don't hear any hit songs here," or as one crass producer bluntly put it, "I am not impressed."

We had what we felt was a God-honoring dream, but our dream of a world-impacting musical ministry went down the drain, helped along by Christians in positions of "authority" whose opinions we respected.

Dashed dreams hurt . . . badly. Through the years, I have counseled with hundreds of sincere believers who could tell similar stories. The details change, but the disillusionment is the same—deep and damaging.

Why does God allow such things to happen? How do you account for those dashed dreams that seemed to be so central to the fulfillment of God's purposes in your life? Can anyone really pick up the pieces of a shattered dream and put it back together?

Tough questions. In attempting to answer them, let's first look at three common mistakes that are sure to lead to dashed dreams and spiritual disillusionment: misguided mentors, misconceptions about ministry and improper motives.

Misguided Mentors

When seeking, receiving and evaluating spiritual counsel, it is wise to remember that we all "see in a mirror dimly" (1 Corinthians 13:12). Sometimes even the best spiritually-minded advisors offer wrong counsel. No doubt that is one reason the Bible instructs us to seek wisdom from a number of sources before making a decision.

The friends and spiritual leaders who encouraged my brothers and me to pursue a national ministry were well-intentioned but wrong. Fortunately, we never abandoned our initial plan of reaching people with the gospel within a regional ministry, and the Lord continued to honor our efforts. Our dream, though badly tattered, remained intact. The disillusionment for us was not so much that "something good" had failed to happen, but rather that we had so poorly interpreted the Lord's leading. After all, we had fasted and prayed, and still we apparently misread the signals and signs.

Something similar happened to Joe and Marcy. But for them, following the advice of a misguided mentor not only destroyed their dream, it also caused their marriage of eleven years to end in divorce. The couple had sought out their pastor's opinion on a business venture they were considering.

They wanted to purchase a pizza shop and use it as a means of reaching teenagers with the gospel. They would play Christian music and pass out gospel literature with every pizza. The pastor was a sincere, godly man but had little business acumen. Still, he encouraged Joe and Marcy to "take a leap of faith" and plunge into the pizza business. He prayed a lovely prayer over the couple and pronounced the Lord's blessing upon their venture.

Teeming with confidence, Joe and Marcy sold their assets and purchased the business, truly believing that God was going to "bless" their efforts. In their minds, that meant He would financially as well as spiritually prosper the business.

Six months later, Joe and Marcy realized they had made a serious mistake. They were in debt over their heads with no apparent escape except bankruptcy. Financial pressures created stress and strain in other areas of their relationship and before long the cracks began to show.

Both blamed each other for getting involved in the foolish investment. As Marcy watched their life savings spiral down the drain, her nerves gave way. Prone to nervous overreaction anyhow, she began smoking cigarettes again, a habit from which she had been delightfully delivered shortly after entrusting her life to Christ. Soon "her nerves" were causing her to smoke three packs a day.

Joe and Marcy's spiritual lives slid drastically downhill since the business allowed so little time for church activities. Their sexual relationship was practically nonexistent due to the long, tedious hours they both worked. Joe, however, managed to muster enough time and energy to carry on an illicit affair with a female employee several years younger than Marcy.

When Marcy found out, the pizza hit the fan.

Physically exhausted, spiritually depleted, emotionally spent and beleaguered by debts, the couple decided to ditch the dream and get a divorce. When their pastor learned of their decision, he indirectly but publicly condemned them from the pulpit. Neither of them returned to church again.

Misguided mentors: If you listen to them, you may be letting yourself in for a real mess.

Misconceptions About Ministry

Another frequent source of disillusionment associated with dashed dreams can be directly traced to misconceptions about ministry. Frankly, most twentieth-century Christians have a naive concept about the cost of discipleship. Inundated by images of glitz, glitter and glamour generally associated with modern-day televangelism, few Christians have genuine role models. And most fail to realize the negative influence these false impressions of spirituality have made upon their minds. Not surprisingly, many have dreams of Christian super-stardom rather than Christian servanthood.

Missionary organizations and pastoral search committees are crying out today for recruits who are willing to sacrifice even a marginal amount of their personal comfort in order to bring a lost soul into the kingdom of God. Meanwhile, most of us are preoccupied with building our own material kingdoms. Anything that demands sacrifice or impinges upon our personal dreams of success is shunned. To deny oneself, take up the cross and follow Jesus is rapidly becoming a forgotten construct of Christianity.

Somehow, modern Christians have been duped into believing that the Christian life, and Christian ministry in particular, is meant to be a bowl of cherries with no pits, a bed of roses with no thorns, all honey and no bees. Of course, we know better, but deep down we persist in believing that if we ever really get it together with God, we can be another spiritual success story.

Recently a sincere Christian mother confided, "I should never have taught my kids to turn the other cheek. They have turned the other cheek all their lives and where has it gotten them? People have just used them, taken advantage of them and walked all over them."

I sympathized with her concern for her children, but I said, "I believe you did well to teach them the right response to unprovoked anger and resentment. Perhaps what you failed to teach them was an honest, accurate portrayal of the *results* of turning the other cheek."

Jesus never said that folks would pat us on the back for returning good for evil. In fact, He never even said that *God* would reward us in this life for doing right. He said:

> Blessed are you when men cast insults at you, and persecute you, and say all kinds of evil against you falsely, on account of Me. Rejoice, and be glad, for your reward in heaven is great (Matthew 5:11,12).

We've all seen movies in which the star turns the other cheek and, instead of a battle, men and women begin to sing together in beautiful harmony. That's the way it is *supposed* to work. Whenever I have turned the other cheek, though, I've gotten slapped on both sides of my face. When I've offered my shirt to someone who has asked for my jacket, he's taken both my jacket and my shirt. Whenever I've gone the second mile, I have often ended up looking for a ride home.

But lack of tangible results should not prevent us from obeying Christ's commands! We need to be obedience-oriented rather than results-oriented. Otherwise, whenever we do right and get kicked in the face for it, we will become disillusioned.

Eric Liddell, the famous runner upon whom the Academy Award-winning film *Chariots of Fire* was based, walked away from the celebrity and luxury of an athletic career in order to serve the Lord as a missionary in China. But instead of leading thousands to Christ, a Japanese soldier led Liddell into a concentration camp where he died of a brain tumor.

Liddell's story doesn't harmonize with many modern concepts of ministry. Oh, the *Chariots of Fire* part does: Everyone's heart is lifted by the champion runner's uncompromising refusal to run on the Sabbath. But that last part befuddles us. Pouring out your life on a mission field? And then, not even fulfilling your dream as a missionary but dying in ignominious defeat as a prisoner? Where is the glory in that?

God never said the race would be easy; He said run! Eric Liddell, whose motto was "Absolute surrender," said, "When I run, I sense His pleasure!" That's all that matters.

Oswald Chambers, the great devotional writer, could have been speaking for Eric Liddell when he wrote:

> There is only one thing God wants of us and that is our unconditional surrender. . . . [and] simple perfect trust in God, such trust that we no longer want God's blessings, but only want Himself. Have we come to the place where God can withdraw His blessings and it does not affect our trust in Him?[1]

Would that there were more modern-day Christians with that sort of unconditional commitment and dedication! Jesus never called His disciples under false pretenses: "Come follow Me; get your name up in lights; live a life of luxury and pleasure!" Quite the opposite. He said, "If they persecuted Me, they will also persecute you" (John 15:20). He did promise, though, that He would never leave or forsake you, even should awful, unexplainable circumstances strike your life.

In her book *Keep Climbing,* Gail MacDonald tells a story about her friend Linda, a New England pastor's wife, who was washing her clothes in the basement of her home when a man entered the cellar door and, without a word, began to stab her until she fell virtually lifeless to the floor. Her husband, Rich, was at a church meeting, and when he returned home, he found Linda alive but unconscious. For days, her life hung in the balance.

> To this day, the assailant has never been identified. But Linda has survived and has returned to health. When people have said to her, "God was so good to have spared you," Linda replies, "God is good whether I had lived or died."[2]

Improper Motives

Most of us would have a tough time admitting that our motives are impure, but the possibility should be considered when dreams remain unfulfilled, especially those dreams that supposedly have been born out of a desire to do something great for God.

I was once waxing eloquent about some of my ministerial dreams when my older brother, John, decimated me with a question. He asked, "What have you *ever* done for anybody that you did not anticipate something in return?"

At first, I protested loudly at his subtly veiled accusation of manipulation, self-promotion and personal aggrandizement. After all, I was a dedicated Christian. I had poured out my life for Christ. I was serving the Lord (I thought) with all of my heart. But like the great Methodist preacher, Henry Clay Morrison, "My heart was in the ministry, but there was uncleanness in my heart."

Upon reflection, I began to examine my heart-attitudes. Did I truly preach the gospel with pure motives, to see people come to know Christ? Or did I simply enjoy the approval I received from presenting a powerful message? Was I giving the Lord my time, talents and treasures out of a heart of love and gratitude toward Him? Or did I view my good deeds as bargaining chips with God? Was I genuinely concerned about the poor, the downtrodden, the homeless, helpless and hopeless? Or were they merely current Christian causes to champion? Down the list of my so-called "spiritual" activities I went, meticulously dissecting the "why" and not simply the "what" of my busy schedule. Then I turned the same searchlight on my lofty dreams and aspirations.

The results shocked me. I had to admit that many of my current activities and my future dreams were not primarily to glorify God, but to glorify *me*, to make my life more comfortable and more convenient, or to impress other people with my own "greatness" and my many Christian virtues.

John's question had jolted me into the realization of my impure motivation. As I repented, the Lord forgave me and restored in me a right attitude. It felt good to be back where I belonged.

If your dreams have been dashed, or if it seems that they are unduly delayed, give your motives a good going over. You might be surprised at what you find.

Dream On

While the above cautions are still fresh in your mind,

let me be quick to emphasize that ordinarily God *wants* to fulfill your dreams! And His dream for you is even greater than your own.

I can almost hear you saying, "Oh, yeah? If that's so, then what's the problem?"

In his book, *Living With Your Dreams,* Dr. David Seamands explains:

> Our dreams, aspirations, and visions are often God-given and are one of His ways of communicating with us. Through them He wants to develop and use our uniqueness and gifts to accomplish His purposes.
>
> But those dreams can become mixed with our own pride, selfishness, immaturity and sin, and need to be purified, tested, matured, refined, and sometimes even refashioned.
>
> Furthermore, in this fallen, imperfect world these dreams are often interrupted, broken, shattered, and unfulfilled. This can happen through the sins and choices of others, events and circumstances over which we have no control, our own sins and wrong choices, or by a combination of these factors.
>
> When this happens God does not want us to abandon those dreams, but will lovingly work with us to refine our unrealistic dreams, to restore our broken dreams, to realize our delayed dreams, and to redesign our shattered dreams so both *His purposes* and *our dreams* can be fulfilled.[3]

But what about those dreams that defy fulfillment? What then?

5

When Your Dreams Have Gone Down the Drain

If you truly are going to trust God for His best, then you must recognize that He is able to use even dream-dashers for your good.

That guy makes me so mad, I could deck him!" Pete roared as he slammed his briefcase onto the kitchen table.

"What guy?" his wife, Susan, asked.

"My boss. That's what guy. He passed over me again for a promotion. In my place, he promoted the guy I have been training for the past six months. He seems to be doing everything he can to keep me from getting ahead in this company."

"Why would he do that?"

"I don't know. I think he's trying to make me mad enough to quit. He knew I wanted that position. I've worked hard for it. I've earned a promotion. But I'm never going to get anywhere as long as that stumbling block of a boss is in my way."

"Or as long as you have that chip on your shoulder," Susan answered with a slight smile.

"Yeah, I guess you're right," Pete replied as he

slumped into a chair at the table. "But that job was my dream. How am I supposed to go back there when my boss keeps blasting me out of the water? And why should I work so hard just so someone else can use me as a stepping stone? I don't think I'll ever again have the same desire that I once had."

How can you overcome the discouragement and disillusionment from dashed, damaged or destroyed dreams and dare to dream again? Here are four suggestions that will help.

1. Don't Allow Yourself to Get Bitter

Blame kills and bitterness blinds your vision. Resentment and revenge for something somebody said or did in your past will only rob you of your joy today and ruin God's plan for your tomorrows. Furthermore, it is impossible to maintain a right relationship with God when you willfully tolerate unforgiveness in your heart.

Jesus left no room for discussion on this issue. He said:

> For if you forgive men for their transgressions, your heavenly Father will also forgive you. But if you do not forgive men, then your Father will not forgive your transgressions (Matthew 6:14,15).

But what do you do when your dream has been destroyed due to the actions or attitudes of a Christian brother or sister?

The question sounds a lot like Peter when he asked Jesus, "Lord, how often shall my brother sin against me and I forgive him? Up to seven times?" (Matthew 18:21) No doubt, Peter felt that he was being magnanimously spiritual at this point. After all, to forgive the same person seven times . . . what more could one expect?

I can imagine Peter's look of relief when Jesus answered, "No, Peter."

Peter must have thought self-righteously, *Whew! Well I certainly didn't think so!*

But then Jesus burst Peter's spiritual bubble when He said, "I do not say to you, up to seven times, but up to seventy times seven" (18:22).

I doubt that the number 490 has any super-spiritual significance. Nevertheless, in my ministry to disillusioned Christians, I have discovered that inevitably the disillusioned person has been keeping score. Some have lists, journals or diaries filled with wrongs suffered at the hands of the dream-dashers.

In reality, Jesus was telling Peter that no limits are allowed when it comes to forgiveness. He is saying the same to you.

Keep in mind, though, forgiveness does not mean condoning sin, overlooking a wrong done or pretending the offense never happened. Nor is it excusing or rationalizing the sin into a sort of psychological purgatory. True forgiveness recognizes the sin, the wrong and the hurt that was inflicted, but *chooses* to let go and never raise the issue again.

Forgiveness: It's not just forgive and forget; it's forgive or forget it! If God has forgiven you, you have no right to withhold forgiveness from someone else.

If there have been individuals, groups, companies, systems, churches or whatever that have had a helping hand in damaging your dreams, you'll do yourself no favors by holding on to ugly resentments. Acknowledge the hurt and let it go. Choose to forgive. If you refuse to forgive, healing will never happen and you will be stuck in a quagmire of anger, guilt and bitterness.

Sometimes people become bitter over what they *perceive* to be a failure or fault on the part of somone else. Regardless, the results of resentment are the same.

Maryanne and Kelly were best friends for as long as they had known each other. All through high school and college they talked about moving to the city, getting an apartment and opening a business together. They had their dream all planned.

Then one night at a party, Maryanne met Jeff. They were instantly attracted to each other and began dating seriously during Maryanne's senior year of college. Kelly watched helplessly as her best friend and future business partner fell head over heels in love. She wanted to be happy for Maryanne and Jeff, but she couldn't. The way she saw things, Jeff had come between her and Maryanne.

When Maryanne and Jeff announced their engagement, Kelly hit the roof. She lost control and began cursing Maryanne for betraying their friendship and Jeff for interfering in their future. Maryanne tried to console Kelly by pointing out that they could still go into business together, but Kelly wouldn't hear of it.

Maryanne was deeply hurt. Still, her mind was made up: She loved her friend dearly, but she loved Jeff even more. Maryanne and Jeff married the summer following graduation.

Kelly grew distant, hostile and bitter. She blamed Jeff and Maryanne for destroying her dream. Although extremely talented, she bounced aimlessly from one trivial job to another, rarely staying at any place of employment for more than a few months.

To this day, Kelly dwells upon what could have been if only Maryanne and Jeff had not married. She unfairly uses her friend's happy marriage as a lame excuse to rationalize her own lack of motivation and achievement.

One of Kelly's friends says, "Every time the subject of Maryanne and Jeff comes up, Kelly turns into a different person. You almost want to grab her by the shoulders, shake her, and say, 'Come on, Kelly! You've mourned for the dearly departed long enough. It's time to wake up and get on with your life!' "

Self-pity and blame are sure roads to alienation and self-destruction. Self-pity is nothing less than disenchanted egotism. It is pride turned upside down. It's an attitude of, "I didn't get what I wanted when I wanted it, so I think I'll eat some worms!"

When you blame other people, you alienate yourself from them. You become bitter, resentful and filled with a strange poisonous venom that stings the other person and always destroys a part of you in the process. If you blame yourself for your soured dreams, you snuff out your passion, goals and self-worth. If you blame God for your disappointments, you cut yourself off from the one person who can truly help you through your time of trial.

One thing is certain: No matter who you blame for dashing your dreams, *you* get worse rather than better.

Instead of wallowing in self-pity, assessing blame, looking for an excuse or a scapegoat, let go of those past hurts. If you are harboring bitterness, seek forgiveness from the Lord first, then, if possible, from the person you have been resenting. Forget the past and step confidently and freely into the future the Lord has for you.

2. Puncture the Pipedreams

A second suggestion for rebuilding your broken dreams is to *be realistic.* Don't allow anyone to destroy your dreams, but don't hang on endlessly to a pipedream either. By definition, a pipedream is an "illusory or fantastic plan, hope or story." It is a dream with no possible fulfillment. While perseverance and tenacity are admirable qualities, so is honesty. Nothing is wrong with saying, "Oops! I made a wrong turn. I've been banging on the door to an empty room."

Understand, when it comes to discerning the will of

God, I believe in knocking on doors. If an opportunity arises that is within biblical boundaries, press on the door a bit. If it opens, step cautiously and prayerfully forward. If it slams in your face, don't try to break the door down!

Certainly, some doors do not even merit your investigation. For example, should you or should you not marry an unbeliever? If you are serious about following Jesus, that door is already closed (see 2 Corinthians 6:14). Don't waste your time praying about marrying an unbelieving partner. Instead, pray for his or her salvation or pray for wisdom on how to tactfully get out of that relationship. Don't ask God to bless what He has already condemned or to open doors He has declared off-limits.

Your heavenly Father knows how to open doors for you. If He could cause the Red Sea to roll back and allow two million of His people to cross on dry ground, He can make a way for you as well, *if* the direction you are heading is the dream He desires to fulfill.

Set realistic goals, seek the Lord's direction and wisdom, and refuse to wallow in past failures.

3. Grow Where You Are Planted

Many Christians have a sad tendency to live on "Someday Isle": *Someday* I'll be successful. *Someday* my prince will come. *Someday* my dreams will come true.

They call their frequent trips to "Someday Isle" journeys of faith. More often than not, their unfulfilled fantasies can be attributed to foolishness, procrastination or laziness. It's time to get real. Why should God open a door of greater opportunity and responsibility if you are not doing your best to use what He has already given you?

A friend of mine says she would love to use her artistic ability for the Lord, but she never does. She has dreams of her art on Christian book jackets, album covers, posters and other professional products. When I suggested to her she could also use her ability for the Lord by designing sets for the church Christmas cantata, or helping with the church newsletters, or volunteering to teach a class at the local Christian school, she looked at me and said pompously, "But Ken, I am an artist."

I wanted to reply, "Yeah, and a proud, selfish, lazy one, too!" but I held my tongue and mumbled some spiritual sounding gibberish about how I was sure the Lord would open up opportunities at the right time. Hey, what are friends for? (I later repented for lying.)

Do you want to sing or play an instrument for the Lord? Then volunteer to sing in the church choir or play for the youth camp. Don't just sit around waiting for your pastor to have a midnight vision informing him that you have ability. Volunteer.

Do you want to be involved in a youth program or senior citizens program or some other worthwhile project? Jump in with both feet! Get involved. Find a need and fill it. Keep your eyes open for the needs of others, and you will always have a ministry.

Do you have some special gift or talent you would like to use for God's glory? Then do it! Opportunities abound in the church and in civic groups for the person who wants to give something back.

But beware of looking for pay or pats on the back. If you wouldn't do what you love without pay or applause, you will probably never *be* paid or appreciated for doing it.

When it comes to your gifts, talents and abilities, the old saying is right up to date: "Either use it or lose it." It is a principle of life: The person who faithfully gives what he or she has will receive more; the person who hoards his or her resources will lose it all.

One of the great Old Testament stories is that of Joseph. Many lessons can be learned from a study of his life, but one of the most telling episodes occurred when he was a prisoner in Egypt. Pharaoh's cupbearer and baker were thrown in the same prison as Joseph and both men had disturbing dreams. Now comes the intriguing part:

> When Joseph came to them in the morning and observed them, behold they were dejected. And he asked . . . "Why are your faces so sad today?" (Genesis 40:6,7)

It may well be that the greatest miracle was not that Joseph was later able to interpret their dreams, but that he noticed the dejection in their faces. Remember, Joseph was also in prison, incarcerated on an unjust charge, yet he still was sensitive to the needs of others and he felt compassion for them (Genesis 39:20-23).

Regardless of your own damaged dream, if you stay sensitive to the needs of others, your turn will come. And don't wait for a public show. Display your compassion where it counts—in the dark prisons of life.

If your dreams have been damaged, look around and find ways to grow where you have been planted. You'll find that new dreams will soon be sprouting.

4. Keep On Believing!

Believe God for the best. It sounds so simple, doesn't it? Yet the battle in the Christian life is not always between good and bad; more frequently, it is between good and *best*.

We often protest, "God, I know what I want!"

The Lord must smile at our immaturity as He responds, "Yes, I know that you think you know what you want. But I know what you *need*."

If you will trust Him, He *will* work out His plan in your life, regardless of your own failures, foibles and foolishness. That's the easy part to believe.

The tough part is believing that He actually does cause "all things to work together for good to those who love God, to those who are called according to His purpose" (Romans 8:28). *All* things includes sins, mistakes and evil machinations of other individuals who have negatively influenced your life. If you truly are going to trust God for His best, then you must recognize that He is able to bless and use even dream-dashers for your good.

One of my spiritual heroes is Samuel Logan Brengle, the brilliant but humble Salvation Army Commissioner whose books on holiness have been a source of spiritual blessing to millions of readers. One night in Boston, a drunken thug hurled a brick at Brengle as he stood in the doorway of the Salvation Army building. The man was barely ten feet away so the brick blasted full force into Brengle's head, smashing it into the doorpost.

For weeks, the preacher who had laid his life on the line to help the poor and needy lay in limbo between life and death at the hands of one to whom he had come to minister. As a result of the blow, Brengle was incapacitated for more than eighteen months. For the rest of his life, he experienced recurring bouts of depression and intense headaches that his doctors attributed to the blow from the brick.

During his recuperation, Brengle kept busy by writing articles for *The War Cry,* a Salvationist magazine. Later, those articles were collected into a short but powerful book, *Helps to Holiness.* The book was an instant success. The little volume was distributed around the world and translated into dozens of languages. It continues to be an encouraging guide for many Christians searching for a deeper walk with Christ.

Whenever people complimented Brengle or thanked him for the blessing that his book had been to them, Brengle would smile and say, "Well, if there had been no little brick, there would have been no little book!"

His optimistic outlook was shared by his wife, Lily.

One day Brengle found Lily painting a biblical text on the very brick that had been used to assault him. The inscription was the word of and confidence in God's plan that Joseph had spoken to his brothers who had sold him into slavery; "You meant it for evil; but God meant it for good . . ."[1] God can do the same with the bricks that have battered you.

The Bible doesn't say that all of those evil things that have happened to you *are* good; it says God *causes* all things to work together for your good. You can trust Him, even when it seems your dreams are going down the drain.

Early in my new Christian life, I became discouraged because God was not answering my prayers the way I thought He should. I asked my pastor why God was holding out on me. He smiled calmly and proceeded to teach me a simplistic limerick that has helped me through some rough spots. He said:

> If the *request* is wrong, God will say, "No."
> If the *timing* is wrong, God will say, "Slow."
> If *you* are wrong, God will say, "Grow!"

Country music crooner Garth Brooks puts it similarly in song. In lamenting the girl who got away, Garth looks at his wife and realizes, "Some of God's greatest gifts are unanswered prayers."

That's it, isn't it? Part of the secret to overcoming spiritual disillusionment is believing that God gives only good gifts to His children, that He will bring into your life only that which is *best* for you, and that He will turn those seemingly negative experiences into something beautiful.

Who wouldn't want to trust a God like that?

6

Disappointment With Other Christians

*Is there anything worse than disappointment
in a brother or sister?*

A friend of mine became involved in a business dispute between himself and a fellow Christian which required litigation between the partners. At his first appearance in the court chambers, my friend told the judge he did not wish to sue his partner.

"Why not?" the judge wanted to know.

"Because, I'm a Christian," my friend began slowly, his normally booming voice barely a whisper, "and I believe the Bible teaches that two Christians should settle their differences outside of court."

The judge threw back his head and howled in laughter. Then his tone turned caustic. "Listen, son," he said, "that's okay. I try cases between Christians in here all the time. When it comes to money, they leave their Christianity back there at the door."

My friend left that day disillusioned . . . and with a lawsuit, initiated by a brother in Christ.

One of the major stumbling blocks to spiritual growth,

as well as one of the main causes of spiritual disillusionment, is our disappointment with other Christians. Multitudes of witnesses could be called at this point—sadly, enough to fill entire volumes.

Is there anything worse than disappointment in a brother or sister? Especially when their attitude or actions directly affect your own dreams and plans?

The scars of disillusionment run deeply when the wounds are inflicted by a friend. Russ and Elizabeth and Jerry and Karen were not mere friends; they were *best* friends. They did everything together. They went to church together, served on committees together, vacationed together and babysat each other's children.

When Karen's doctor diagnosed her as having cancer, nobody was surprised that Elizabeth and Russ were at her bedside along with Jerry.

Karen's condition deteriorated rapidly, but she refused to be admitted to the hospital. "If the Lord wants to heal me, He can do it just as easily at home," she said.

Elizabeth visited Karen every day. Often she and Russ would make a cake or a pie or a meal and take it to their friends. Jerry greatly appreciated their kindness, lavishly expressing his gratitude to Elizabeth, although Karen rarely was able to eat much. Each evening, before they left for home, Russ, Elizabeth, Jerry and Karen all held hands and prayed together around the bedside.

Karen's ordeal wore on. She became less and less communicative and Jerry became more and more despondent. Elizabeth decided it was her duty to console him, which she did. Too well. Before long, Elizabeth and Jerry were entangled in a full-blown affair, while Jerry's wife lay in the next room fighting for her life.

Karen seemed to sense her husband's unfaithfulness, but she lacked the will and the physical energy to do much about it. She never dreamed he was sleeping with her best friend. In her weakness she knew she was unable to meet Jerry's sexual needs and was tempted to condone his actions. Still, they had vowed "for better or for worse" on their wedding day. Didn't that mean anything at all?

Jerry and Elizabeth increasingly flaunted their affair. Soon, other people in town were guessing what was going on during Elizabeth's frequent house calls. When Russ first heard the rumors, he defiantly defended his wife's honor and that of his friend. But two weeks after Karen's death, Elizabeth filed for divorce and Russ was devastated. He simply could not believe that his wife would do something so despicable against God, her dying friend and him. Neither could he fathom why his best friend would so willfully deceive him.

Elizabeth and Jerry moved in together in a town twenty miles down the road. Russ became a recluse, refusing to return to church and rarely coming out of the house. He rationalized, "If I can't trust my wife and my best friend whom I can see, how can I trust a God I can't see?" Good question.

What good could possibly come from such things? Why does God allow them to happen? David Seamands believes: "It is to teach us full dependence on Himself through *the discipline of detachment* from others."[1] Maybe so. But that still doesn't take away the pain.

Millions of men and women became disillusioned Christians following the infamous televangelism scandals of 1987. Some are still reeling and are having difficulty recovering. One elderly, devout man spoke for many when he commented, "My goodness! Who can you trust anymore? I mean, they preached the gospel with such authority."

The sad truth is, millions of Christians did trust these men of God. Many put their money where their hearts were, too. Horror stories abound of senior citizens and struggling young couples who donated thousands of dollars to these ministries, only to become disillusioned Christians in the aftermath of the televangelists' improprieties.

Snakes in the Church!

I have served on ecumenical pastor committees which were called together for the sole purpose of reaching a particular area with the gospel. On more occasions than I care to disclose, the group disbanded its efforts over some extremely minor point: the location of the public services, whether the auditorium lights should be on or off, what type of music would be sung. Not once, in my experience, was the divisive issue the blood of Christ or what a man or woman must do to be saved. Apparently, we all agreed on the basics. Or maybe we just never got that far.

One of the most disillusioning points about the pastorate is the inability of pastors to work together for the glory of Christ. When spiritual leaders do cooperate, it makes the news, and not necessarily because of some great outbreak of revival (although that is often the result), but because the clergy so rarely crosses its own manmade barriers.

Oh, yes, we can occasionally lay down our differences long enough to march in protest against something that nearly all Christians perceive as reprehensible, like abortion or pornography. But even then, the numbers of participants are minuscule compared to the potential represented by believers.

Thankfully, courageous exceptions are springing up in many communities. Pastors and congregations are beginning to realize that the enemy is not the church down the street—those people are the allies. The enemy is Satan and his demonic cohorts.

Still, the body of Christ consistently has difficulty

posting a united front.

I've always had a fairly good handle on persecution of Christians by "the world." Jesus said to expect it, so I do. But I've never been able to figure out why Christians are so cruel and callous toward each other. Why do God's people continually hurt God's people?

Once, during an open congregational meeting, I watched in stunned silence as members tore into their church leaders, hurling insults back and forth across the crowded room. The leaders responded in kind, and before long the church meeting threatened to turn into a prizefight.

It was one of the few times in my life when I have been speechless. All I could think was, *So this is the seamless body of Christ?* Maybe I should have said that.

For six years I served a church as "acting senior pastor," a purposely obscure title. The church had experienced a devastating congregational split prior to my tenure and the aftershock hit shortly after my arrival. The divisive issue was, "Who's in charge around here?" The elders? The pastors? Or the congregation? People took sides, and some families split down the middle.

I stepped into a situation that was similar to a snake pit. People were hissing at each other, ready to strike with little provocation. Just after I got there, someone told me they had had a vision in which they had seen the church building with this epitaph over it: "Ichabod, Ichabod," meaning "the glory of the Lord is departed." Not exactly the sort of welcoming committee a pastor loves to see.

Other people told me that the church was under a curse of the devil, or was it a curse of God? They weren't quite sure. But they were convinced the church was cursed.

Oddly, once I grew to know the people of that church and many of the people who had left the church over the schism, I soon found that they were, for the most part, lovely, sincere people who wanted to serve Christ but just couldn't do so together.

The congregation was extremely "normal": a few people with power, prestige, money or clout; some extremely talented, artistic folks; and a large number of common, everyday folks such as you and me. The church was not demon-possessed, cursed of the devil or God, or destined for doom. The church is, after all, only the building. *People* who love Jesus Christ make up Christ's body in that building.

Sadly, church splits inevitably spawn a batch of disillusioned Christians. I've known churches to divide over where the pulpit should sit, what color the carpet should be, or what time the services should start. My friend Mike Warnke says he knows a church that split over the question of whether Adam had a navel. Think about it.

When the Church Lets You Down

More devastating than corporate disillusionment with the church is the personal disappointment that results when people in your fellowship let you down. When people you trust, or in whom you believe, fail to live up to your expectations or fail to be there when you need them, the normal response is a feeling of abandonment, the sense that nobody really cares.

Frequently, your fellow Christians simply miss the fact that you are hurting. They don't recognize your need, and therefore make no attempt to minister to you. Sometimes, however, the reason for ignoring your pain is more sinister. Such was the case with Janice and Steve, a Christian couple actively involved in their local church.

Both Janice and Steve married on the rebound from broken relationships. Their marriage began in the pits and slid downhill from there. Ten years and four children later, they were still living together as husband and wife, but their marriage was in shambles.

Early in the relationship, Steve began venting his anger and frustration on Janice. At first, he restricted his abuse to verbal tirades, criticizing her appearance, accusing her of laziness and complaining that she spent too much of his hard-earned money on unnecessary items. Before long his rantings turned to rage and he began physically abusing his wife, pummelling her with his fists until portions of her fair skin turned into ugly, red, blue and purple bruises.

All the while Janice and Steve maintained appearances at church. Although not a paid staff member, Steve was the youth leader and choir director and Janice helped him by playing the piano. They often sang duets together on the church's weekly local television broadcast.

Occasionally, however, Janice could not perform. In his anger, Steve had punched his wife in her face, and the bruises could not be hidden by the best of makeup.

Janice's family members knew something was wrong, but when they threatened to report Steve to the authorities, Janice always covered for him. She believed that her husband was an anointed man of God, that he had a valid and important ministry to perform, and that somehow, she must have caused his anger or invited his abuse. No amount of persuasion could convince her otherwise.

Nothing changed until the day Steve beat up Janice in front of their nine-year-old daughter. Janice said, "I realized then that he was not only battering me, but he was destroying our children's impressions of marriage as well. I went to our pastor for help."

That's when Janice's nightmare really began. The pastor refused to believe that a fine, upstanding fellow such as Steve would abuse his wife. Nevertheless, at Janice's insistence, the pastor reluctantly agreed to speak to Steve about the matter.

When the three of them met, it was a farce. Steve put on a pious performance and convinced the pastor that Janice was merely emotionally distraught due to the pressures of minding the children. Not wanting to create a scene, or perhaps not wanting to lose his youth leader and choir director, the pastor ignored Janice's objections.

A month later, they were back in the pastor's office again. This time Janice was missing a tooth and her right eye was nearly swollen shut. Steve fabricated a story about how she had fallen off a ladder while cleaning the windows. The pastor asked suspicious questions, but nothing more. Steve continued his work with the youth and the choir.

Janice became a recluse. She rarely went out of the house and when Steve invited the church friends over, she refused to play along with the sham any longer and began telling their friends why. None of their friends or church family members believed her story. They just couldn't imagine their dedicated choir director pounding the daylights out of his wife. Steve still performed his ministry at the church while Janice remained conspicuously absent. The beatings at home, however, continued unabated.

Finally, when Janice could endure no more, she went to the civil authorities. After a hearing, the judge ordered Steve out of the house.

When the church members heard the result of the hearing, they ostracized Janice all the more. Most believed she was maliciously attempting to destroy her husband's ministry. They rallied around Steve and left Janice out in the cold. Nobody asked whether or not the charges against Steve were true.

The judge suggested that Janice seek help from a professional counseling service, which she did. The counselor enrolled her in a support group led by an anti-Christian, humanistic psychologist. The group received Janice with open arms. Ironically, she received the help, comfort and encouragement from the support group that her pastor and fellow Christians failed to provide.

Janice remains in counseling but refuses to return to church, any church. She obstinately declares to anyone who will listen, "Those Christians are all a bunch of hypocrites."

Steve never did undergo any rehabilitation program and continues to lead the choir and youth group at church.

When the church lets you down, the results can be devastating.

Unfulfilled Expectations

Sometimes a person perceives that a pastor, church or particular ministry has failed him, when in fact, it is his unrealistic, and therefore unfulfilled, expectations that created the disillusionment.

For example, when Bill and Dottie received a substantial insurance settlement after an auto accident, they decided to give the money to a well-known, reputable ministry in their area. They scheduled a meeting with ministry representatives to arrange for the donation to be handled in the wisest manner.

Nobody coerced Bill and Dottie to give anything. They willingly initiated the meeting and had several months to rescind their offer while the lawyers worked out the details. Ministry officials stressed to them that they did not have any spiritual obligation to give the money away—the money was theirs. Bill and Dottie insisted that they wanted the money to go to the Lord's work and signed over the entire amount to the ministry.

The ministry graciously acknowledged the couple's gift, sending several representatives to visit them with personal thanks and presenting them both publicly and privately with plaques and other tokens of their appreciation. The funds were incorporated into the ministry budget and dispersed into the Lord's work, just as Bill and Dottie had directed.

For more than a year, the couple basked in the glow of their generosity. Then the economy turned sour. Bill was laid off at work and Dottie was forced to return to the workplace in order to make ends meet. Their generous attitude eventually turned as sour as the economy. At first, they merely regretted that they had given their insurance settlement away. Then, as times grew tougher, they began to resent giving the gift to the ministry. They began making snide, derogatory remarks to friends about how "that ministry had ripped off their life savings."

Although representatives from the ministry met with them, as did their own pastor, Bill and Dottie remained rankled. Unfortunately, the funds had already been spent—for the very purposes that the donors had specified—and the ministry could not afford to return funds from their operating expenses. Nor were they legally obligated or advised to do so.

Bill and Dottie's pastor pointed out that, like Barnabas of old, the couple could have done whatever they pleased with the money. But once it was given, it was given to the Lord to be used as the ministry saw fit. And they had no further claims upon it. He also cautioned them against the attitude and actions that destroyed Ananias and Sapphira. Yet in Bill and Dottie's minds, the ministry had taken advantage of their spiritual sensitivities.

"But you didn't have to give the money!" their pastor protested.

"Well they didn't have to take it, either," the couple countered. To this day, Bill and Dottie blame the ministry for their disillusionment and they attempt to discredit the organization any way possible.

Bill and Dottie's disillusionment is their own fault. They should admit their folly and their false accusations and seek forgiveness from all the parties involved. They will never be free until they do.

Unfortunately, many other believers have been legitimately disillusioned by their spiritual leaders.

What To Do When Your Spiritual Leaders Let You Down

Let's face it. Spiritual leaders are human beings, too. They make mistakes, sometimes major mistakes. Most of them mean well, but sometimes they blow it. No Christian leader is infallible.

When a spiritual leader disappoints you, how should you respond?

First, understand that the church is similar to a hospital. It is not a refrigerator to preserve the saints. It is a place where real, bruised, battered and beaten people come to find relief from the pressures of daily life. In any hospital, competent doctors, nurses, medical assistants and a plethora of volunteers are required in order to dispense proper care. Nevertheless, the number of sick and injured patients normally outnumbers the "well" people.

So it is in your church. Your pastor is like the skilled physician. He must treat the immediate need and move on to the next emergency. Other members on his staff, professional or volunteer, administer further assistance if it's needed. In this age of increasing physical distance between the pastor and the people, routine, non-emergency, pastoral visitation is rapidly becoming a ritual of the past.

Keep in mind that other people in your fellowship are hurting, too. Never be reluctant to seek out the help you need, but after you "recuperate," allow the Lord to use you as an instrument of health, healing and encouragement to someone else.

Second, pursue the scriptural pattern for dispelling

disputes and bringing sinful behavior to light. Jesus said:

> And if your brother sins, go and reprove him in private; if he listens to you, you have won your brother.
>
> But if he does not listen to you, take one or two more with you, so that by the mouth of two or three witnesses every fact may be confirmed.
>
> And if he refuses to listen to them, tell it to the church; and if he refuses to listen even to the church, let him be to you as a Gentile and a tax-gatherer (Matthew 18:15-17).

Notice the progression: Go personally to the one with whom you have a dispute. If that accomplishes nothing, take one or more witnesses. If you are still unable to settle your differences, bring the matter before the church. In most cases, this could be a representative body, such as a board of deacons or elders, but some instances may merit a congregational meeting. If you still cannot reach an amicable agreement, and you know your own heart is right in the matter, you are to part company with the recalcitrant brother or sister. Nowhere, however, does Scripture command you to drag his or her name through the mud, broadcast the sin, or allow bitterness in your heart and mind toward the person who has offended you.

Third, pray for the person who has hurt you. It sounds simple enough, doesn't it? But you know better. It is downright difficult to pray for a brother or sister with whom you disagree, or worse, whom you perceive as having damaged you or your loved ones in some way. Still, the command of Jesus is clear:

> But I say to you who hear, love your enemies, do good to those who hate you, bless those who curse you, pray for those who mistreat you. . . . And if you love those who love you, what credit is that to you? For even sinners love those who love them (Luke 6:27,28,32).

Ouch, Jesus! Why did You have to be so specific?

When Your Loved Ones Let You Down

Perhaps nothing hurts worse than when the ones you love the most disappoint you.

At the conclusion of the morning worship service, Margery and George, two pillars of the church, were lamenting to friends about their prodigal son, Ricky.

"We are at our wit's end," Margery said. "We don't know what else to do for Ricky. We raised him right, brought him to church every time the doors were open and sent him off to a Christian college. But he wanted to transfer to the state university. So what could we do? He's old enough to make his own decisions."

"He joined a fraternity and I know he's drinking and carousing and running around with the wrong crowd," George growled angrily. "That boy makes me so mad, I could . . . "

"All we can do is pray," Margery cut him short. "And we do. We pray every day that Ricky will come to his senses."

"Be glad you still have a son to pray for," a compassionate voice said behind them. Margery and George whirled around to see Craig and Connie White standing there smiling at them. The surprise on Margery and George's face quickly turned to embarrassment. They knew all too well what the Whites had been through with their teenage daughter.

Connie and Craig, a devout Christian couple in their mid-forties, loved their three children with all their heart. But for some reason, seventeen-year-old Marsha had pulled away from the family. Marsha complained bitterly each time her parents reprimanded her for coming in late from her dates. She balked at attending church services and sulked around the house whenever Connie and Craig required her to join in family functions.

Marsha's self-image was extremely fragile, bolstered only by her friend's approval and the dubious distinction of being the only girl in her high school who had beaten a rap for possession of marijuana. She neglected to acknowledge that a major reason the judge had let her off was because of her strong family support.

When Marsha began dating Curt, the sparks really began to fly at home. Curt was a known drug dealer in town. He had narrowly missed being sent to juvenile reform school for assaulting a parent of a young lady he had gotten pregnant. He was a heavy drinker and drove a black, beat-up Chevy pickup with obscene pictures painted on its sides.

"That boy is no good for you!" Craig roared when he found out his daughter had been with Curt.

"That's what you say!" Marsha countered.

"That's right! That's exactly what I say," continued Craig. "I'll tell you what else I say: You stay away from that kid, or else!"

"Or else what?" Marsha spat back at him.

"Or else, you're grounded for the rest of the school year."

"So ground me. Big deal. You still can't keep me from seeing Curt at school."

Craig knew that Marsha was right, but he decided to throw down the gauntlet anyhow. "All right, you're grounded!" he bellowed. "For the rest of the school year, I want you in this house before dark every night. And don't even ask to go out on any dates."

Marsha rolled her eyes and shrugged her shoulders as she turned and tiptoed pixie-like toward the television. "Yes, Daddy dear," she sneered.

If she was a boy I'd belt her one, thought Craig as he watched her go.

Craig and Connie held firm on the grounding of their daughter. No dates, no phone calls, no after school activities, and most importantly, no contact with Curt. Marsha remained incorrigible. Craig and Connie prayed for her constantly and regularly requested prayer for her in church. For a while it seemed their sanctions were working.

Then one day, Craig received an emergency phone call at work.

"Mr. White?" a formal, yet nervous sounding voice asked.

"Yes, this is Craig White."

"Mr. White, this is Chief Reynolds of the police department. We need you to come down to the school right away. There has been an accident."

"What?" Craig screamed into the receiver. "What is it?"

"I think you better just hurry on down here," the chief repeated.

Craig raced to his car, dove behind the wheel and stamped the gas pedal down to the floor. The vehicle roared out of the parking lot, the tires spitting gravel into the air behind them.

As Craig careened into the school parking lot, he first saw the flashing red lights. Then his heart sank as he saw the focus of all the attention: a black pickup truck parked next to a wooded area.

He screeched to a stop, threw open the car door and bolted toward the pickup, his own car engine still running.

"I'm Craig White! Chief Reynolds told me there's been an accident. Where? What's going on?"

Chief Reynolds grabbed Craig's shoulder from behind. "You better come with me, Mr. White. We need to talk." He stepped in front of Craig, standing between Craig and the truck, and put both his hands on Craig's shoulders. "It's not an accident, Mr. White. Your daughter and her boyfriend are in that truck. They have committed suicide."

From the moment Craig heard those awful words, his life was never the same. The next few days blurred into a surrealistic nightmare for him and Connie, the details vaguely but indelibly impressed upon their minds: the autopsy, the funeral details, the mourning of friends and family, the funeral itself with many of Marsha's schoolmates in attendance, the nagging, gnawing silence after everyone was gone, and the house with one empty bedroom . . .

"Be thankful you have a son to pray for, George," Craig repeated. "We'll never know the condition of our daughter the day she stepped into eternity, but you still have a chance to reach Ricky. Don't give up on him. Keep praying for him. Keep encouraging him. Keep building bridges into his world. Don't expect him to walk a tightrope back into yours.

"After Marsha took her life," Craig went on, "Connie and I dropped out of everything. For three years, I could barely function. I got fired from two jobs and felt like killing myself. I couldn't force myself to come back to this church, even though the people here loved us and continually poured out their kindness and compassion on us.

"Then one day the Lord spoke to me, gently but firmly. The thought kept running through my head, *How long are you going to wallow in self-pity? You aren't mourning for Marsha anymore. You're mourning for yourself.* I knew it was a word from God. I couldn't get away from it. Then and there, I asked God to make me into an encourager rather than a mourner."

"It hasn't been easy," added Connie. "We still miss Marsha and the road back has been rugged. But we are committed to loving God, loving our two remaining kids and loving God's people for as long as He gives us breath. Let's pray for your Ricky right now."

Christians are never immune from the tragedies and disappointments of life. You don't always get what you expect or what you deserve. You can't always choose what is going to come your way. But you can choose how you will respond.

Whatever your disappointing situation, you can get out of the pit and begin to live a fruitful, fulfilling life for God's glory. A few simple principles will help you see how to do it.

7

Real-Life Answers for Ripped-Off Believers

*If you've been burned, perhaps it's time to quit
complaining and allow the Lord to bring
healing to your heart.*

We've all known the nasty, horrible sensation in the pit of our stomachs that disappointment brings, especially when the disappointment involves someone you love. The apostle Paul must have felt that way about Demas, his friend and co-worker. Demas deserted the apostle during Paul's final days. You sense the apostle's despair in his letter to Timothy when he says, "Make every effort to come to me soon; for Demas, having loved this present world, has deserted me" (2 Timothy 4:9,10).

What should you do when you are disappointed by loved ones, burned by believers or fried by friends in the fellowship? Five attitude adjustments have helped me dig out from under the disillusioning spiritual doldrums.

1. Conquer Your Cynicism

Cynics believe that everyone is a crook of some kind . . . most just haven't gotten caught. They believe that every human being's conduct is motivated by nothing more than self-interest. Obviously, this attitude can cause you to become a deeply distrustful, pessimistic, contemptuous, fault-finding person. You must conquer cynicism at all cost!

Unfortunately, cynicism is rapidly catching on in America. An article in *Success* magazine (October 1989) reported that according to comprehensive surveys:

> A full 43 percent of American workers fall into the "cynic" category: Not only do they mistrust government, big business, and products they purchase, they are deeply suspicious of their employers, supervisors, and colleagues. Another 16 percent are classified as "wary," with strong cynical leanings. That leaves just 41 percent who can safely be diagnosed as "upbeat": productive, positive, and committed.

Cynical attitudes have infected the church, aided, no doubt, by the aberrant behavior of spiritual leaders from whom we expected more. Nevertheless, as a Christian, it is unnerving when you notice yourself sliding toward cynicism.

Thom Hickling, host of "His Place," a popular Christian television program in Pittsburgh, has every reason to be cynical. His parents own and operate a Christian radio station, and Thom and his wife Cathy publish *Expression*, a Christian newspaper. At one time they promoted Christian concerts. Sadly, Thom and members of his family have been ripped off by the "best" in the business. From radio evangelists who failed to pay their bills, to advertisers who reneged on contracts, to Christian artists who would not perform unless their dressing rooms were supplied with the proper foods and flowers, Thom has seen the best and the worst in Christian circles.

I asked him if he ever felt skeptical.

"Oh, no," he answered quickly. "I'm not skeptical anymore. I tend to be cynical, and that's what scares me." Thom knows that his cynicism could easily be his undoing.

"If I don't keep my cynicism in check," he says, "mistrust moves in, and every conversation is then colored by a doubt of the other person's credibility and integrity."

How can we overcome cynicism? The Gospel of John has some insight. John writes:

> Now when He was in Jerusalem at the Passover, during the feast, many believed in His name. . . . But Jesus, on His part, was not entrusting Himself to them, for He knew all men (John 2:23,24).

Jesus was never astonished by His followers' proclivity toward evil. He never said, "Wow, I really expected better from you folks." On the contrary, He knew their hearts better than they did. He recognized and accepted their potential for the best or the worst behavior, and still He loved them. He never lashed out in caustic cynicism, not even when He condemned the self-righteous Pharisees.

What an example He has given us! Jesus wisely did not entrust Himself to the fickle whims of the crowd, but He never quit loving or helping people to see God's kingdom. Right up to the day He died, He continued to reach out to the people who had rejected Him the most. His example declares loudly to us, "There is no place for cynicism in the kingdom of God."

2. Keep on Loving

Robin Norwood's *Women Who Love Too Much* purports that it is possible to love somebody too much. She writes that love often blinds a person to another person's faults, and therefore opens the door to personal abuse. With all due respect to the bestseller's list, I believe the author of that book is wrong.

Love does not blind; *sin* blinds. Paul says love "bears all things, believes all things, hopes all things, endures all things" (1 Corinthians 13:7), not "Love is blind." Love sees.

Love accepts a person where he or she is, warts and all. Love keeps on loving, even if that person falls on his or her face, an abject failure.

Certainly, I could never condone abuse in a relationship, nor would I counsel a person to remain in a relationship in which abuse is occurring, but nowadays we write off people much too quickly. Jesus didn't write off people. He kept on loving His friends right up to the night they betrayed Him. Can you imagine Jesus sitting at the table at the Last Supper, *knowing* that before the night was over Peter would deny Him three times and the other disciples would head for the hills of Bethany?

And then there was Judas.

Jesus knew what Judas was going to do, but He continued to love him to the end, giving him every opportunity to turn away from his devious destiny. I believe if Judas had come to the foot of the cross after the betrayal and cried out for mercy, Jesus would have forgiven Him.

Nowadays, we blow people off if they don't smile at us in church.

My brother John saw a lonely figure standing in a corner at a busy airport, obviously attempting to avoid detection. John immediately recognized the fellow as a formerly popular Christian recording artist who had publicly stepped away from the Lord and into the secular music scene. He was now rich and famous—and hiding from his fans.

John decided to say hello. To my brother's surprise, the superstar remembered him and even asked about the other members of our family.

They talked for a while and reminisced about the "good old days" until it was time for both of them to board their planes. Before saying good-bye, John said, "I'm really glad I came over to talk to you. When I saw you standing there, I debated whether I should. Now that you're so well known, I figured you'd have people badgering you all the time, especially friends from the old days."

The star's eyes saddened as he replied, "No, that's not the case. As a matter of fact, since I left Christian music, I rarely hear from any of my old buddies. It's like I don't exist anymore. Every once in a while, I'll see someone I recognize from my gospel days at a show, but they never stop to talk. I don't hear from them anymore." Sad song, isn't it?

Never underestimate your heavenly Father's ability and *desire* to forgive and restore a fallen brother or sister.

A number of years ago, two dear, Christian couples, both friends of mine, divorced. Not only did they divorce, but they remarried each other's mate. Brenda married Bruce, Diane's former husband, and Joe, Brenda's former husband, married Diane. Confused? I was too.

More than that, I was outraged and disappointed. I had looked to these couples as spiritual leaders, and in my most self-righteous, Pharisaical attitude, I condemned them: *How could they do such a thing? Don't they know the influence they have upon other people? How could they let me down like this?* I deliberately cut them out of my life.

Nearly twenty years later, long after I had repented of my judgmental attitude, I walked into an extremely conservative church where I was scheduled to speak and was shocked to see Brenda and Bruce sitting in the front row. I knew that before I could speak to anyone else about harboring bitterness or resentment, I had to confess my own failure and ask forgiveness from Brenda and Bruce. They lovingly accepted my apologies and we prayed together before the service began.

They invited me to their home after church and I gladly took them up on their offer. While relaxing with my old friends, I was delighted to discover that God had done a marvelous healing in their hearts. Brenda told me their story.

"After our divorces," she began, "all of us went into spiritual paralysis for a while. We realized we had acted selfishly, ignoring the negative consequences that our actions would have on our children, friends and families. The Lord began dealing with us about the sinful aspects of the divorce as well as a lot of our actions and attitudes that led to divorce.

"As we humbled ourselves and repented, the Lord began a miraculous, restorative process. He showed us that divorce is not the unpardonable sin. I don't mean that He condoned our divorces, but He has picked up the pieces and put us back together again.

"Unfortunately, sin is always costly. We've had trouble with our kids. We've had a terrible strain in our marriage. Diane and Joe didn't make it. They got divorced after a few years. Diane has married again, but Joe has not. He is antagonistic toward God and anything Christian. Their kids are an emotional mess.

"On the positive side, God has restored Bruce and me as individuals and as a couple. Perhaps, even more amazing," Brenda's eyes lit up, "He has given us another opportunity to serve Him. When we first came here, we informed the church elders about our marriage. We thought our divorces might interfere with our future ministry, but the elders said no. The community and the church have been rocked by divorces of influential couples. The elders wanted somebody who knew the pain, but who also knew that God can heal. So here we are!"

Don't ever give up on a person who has disappointed you, hurt you or otherwise let you down. You'd be amazed what God can do.

He still puts up with you, doesn't He?

3. Quit Licking Your Wounds

Okay, you've been hurt. Pardon my bluntness, but welcome to the real world.

Everybody has been let down by somebody. If we are semi-honest, we must confess that we have been a source of disappointment to somebody else as well. Christians fail each other—it's that simple.

So you feel you've been ripped off. Well, how long are you going to rant, rave, pout and whine about it?

Fifteen years ago, Bob and Alice's only son was killed in a freak accident at work. It was one of those senseless, unexplainable accidents for which there are no words of comfort. Family and friends hovered over the couple for several months, empathizing with them in their grief and attempting to nurture them back to a degree of normalcy.

Regardless of the comforters' sensitive efforts, Bob and Alice refused to let go of their grief. Whenever their son's name was mentioned, their eyes welled up with tears and their woeful mourning began all over again. Slowly but surely, the comforters quit coming. People stopped calling. Family members avoided visiting.

Anytime an encourager bravely attempted to lift the couple's spirits, his or her efforts were met with sullen faces and a barrage of insults.

"You just don't know what it is like to lose your only son," Bob objected.

"No, but God does," somebody would tell them.

"Well, that's different," came Alice's retort.

"I understand," said a mother who had lost her husband and three children in a electrical fire in her home. But Bob and Alice remained untouched. In their minds, nobody had ever felt pain the way they had.

No consolation seemed adequate to their need. Consequently, fifteen years after the fact, Bob and Alice continue to wallow in self-pity and self-induced isolation.

If you've been burned, or if unexplainable pain has been part of your life, perhaps it's time to quit complaining and allow the Lord to bring healing to your heart.

An elderly woman reached near celebrity status in 1990 for a single line in a television commercial. "I've fallen," she cried, "and I can't get up!" She was all alone and had nobody to help her. Fortunately, she had purchased an electronic device that enabled her to call for assistance.

In the Bible, there is the story of a man who had been crippled for thirty-eight years. Every day he sat at the Pool of Bethesda in Jerusalem, ostensibly waiting for a miracle to deliver him from his morbid condition. Too bad for him no wonder-gadgets had been invented yet so he could call for help. Rumor had it, however, that every once in a while an angel would descend and stir up the water in the pool, and the first person to step into the stirred waters was healed of whatever disease he or she had. So the crippled man continued to wait.

John tells us, "When Jesus saw him lying there, and knew that he had already been a long time in that condition, He said to him, 'Do you wish to get well?'" (John 5:6)

When I first read that question, I thought, *Jesus, what a joke! Of course, the man wants to be well.* But as I studied this story, I realized the question was not, "Do you think I can make you well?" or "Do you believe I can lift you out of your doldrums?" It was, "Do *you* wish to get well?" Jesus placed the pressure at the most sensitive spot in the man's life—his desire to be healed.

The lame man missed the point and began his usual poor, poor, pitiful me routine: "Sir, I have no man to put me into the pool when the water is stirred up, but while I am coming, another steps down before me" (John 5:7). What was he saying? "Other people have let me down. I can't depend upon anybody around here for help."

That was not the question Jesus had asked. Jesus was not interested in commiserating with someone who wished only to continue living in the past while making excuses for his present. He wanted to heal the man. He said, "Arise, take up your pallet, and walk" (5:8). And the man did.

Two actions are necessary if you want to be well. First, *let go of the past*—those past hurts, disappointments, mistakes, failures and sins. Holding on to grief, resentment, bitterness or negative attitudes will only immobilize you and prevent your healing.

Second, *by an act of your will, get up and step into the great future that Jesus has for you.* You needn't have a huge amount of faith. Apparently the crippled man at the pool had little to none. But when Jesus said, "Arise," he took that first genuine step of faith, and his life was never the same. After thirty-eight years of frustration and futility, he was healed.

4. Accept People Where They Are, Not Where You Want Them to Be

To avoid being disappointed and disillusioned by other people, you must come to grips with your own unrealistic expectations of them. Remember, people are in process; none of us has "arrived" yet. Unless you choose to live life in a shell, you are going to encounter immaturity, insincerity and sin. Yes, even in the lives of fellow believers.

No doubt you have already met your share of users, losers and other abusers. You can wring your hands in frustration and despair, look down your nose in self-righteous condemnation or you can learn to say, "Okay. That's where this person is, and that's the best I can expect from them right now."

Sitting in a restaurant with my family, I could not help

noticing the loud, obnoxious, miscreant boy in the next booth. The child was throwing his food and poking at anyone who passed closely by the table where he and his parents were seated.

Despite his despicable behavior, nobody protested to the restaurant manager. Why? He was a "special child," obviously crippled and mentally deficient. His mind was impaired and his body moved in spasmodic gestures and motions. Nobody expected him to behave like the other little boys, and nobody was surprised or offended by his outbursts.

Sometimes, you must regard the people who have disappointed you as spiritual cripples—not with self-righteous condescension, but like you would react to the rantings and ravings of a special child. Your tolerance level can rise to the need. Instead of responding in anger and bitterness, you are able to look at your offender with compassion and understanding.

Remember, too, that Jesus taught, "Do not judge lest you be judged. For in the way that you judge, you will be judged; and by your standard of measure, it will be measured to you" (Matthew 7:1,2).

We have no right to act as judge, jury and executioner. Who are we to say that another person has exhausted God's mercy and grace? Our heavenly Father is the master potter who specializes in molding, shaping and remaking broken lives. It's our responsibility to keep our attitudes correct by accepting people where they are. We're to keep on loving and forgiving them. The Lord will do the rest.

If you find you cannot be around people who have hurt you or disappointed you without your own heart becoming tainted or callous, it would be better to simply separate for a while. Avoid seeing each other, but leave the door open to reconciliation.

5. The Final Score Hasn't Been Tallied Yet

Sometimes you may be tempted to agree with Jenny, a Christian woman whose husband walked out on her. She grumbled, "Wait a minute. This doesn't make sense. I've been the one trying to do right, to live as a Christian should in these circumstances, and I am paying the price. Meanwhile, my husband seems to be going along just fine, even getting ahead in life."

Whenever you are tempted to succumb to that sort of thinking, remember: The game isn't over yet, and the time of final reckoning is still to come. But it does bring up a sticky issue—one that deserves a chapter of its own.

8

When Good Things Happen to Bad People

"God, why are You withholding Your blessings from me while known pagans are prospering?"

Several years ago, a relatively obscure rabbi by the name of Harold Kushner wrote a book with the appealing title, *When Bad Things Happen to Good People*. More than 500,000 hardback copies sold almost overnight. Since then, literally millions of copies in paperback have sold.

Kushner's book raises the perennial, party-squelching question: "How can a loving God allow such terrible suffering and evil in this world?"

Kushner's question is certainly not novel. Every time I speak at a youth conference, a swaggering teenager will approach me with that "look" in his or her eye. Then, as though brandishing a sword that will forever slice my faith into molecular-sized shreds, he asks the same question: "If God is so good, why does He permit all the bad things in the world?" It always takes a supreme measure of aplomb on my part to treat the question with the seriousness that it merits and—here's the hard part—as though my interrogator were the first to ever consider the Rabbi Kushner-type question.

Granted that Harold Kushner's question is one of the toughest of life to answer, turn it around and it becomes even more difficult. Instead of, "Why do *bad* things happen to *good* people?" consider this: "Why do *good* things happen to *bad* people?"

What in the World Is God Doing?

That was the question Asaph pondered aloud in Psalm 73. Asaph was the man who headed up King David's music ministry. He later did the same for David's son, Solomon. He wrote at least twelve of the psalms and was one of David's top three musicians, along with Heman and Jeduthun.

You first meet Asaph when the Ark of the Covenant is being moved from Obed-Edom to Jerusalem. Asaph was selected as one of the priestly singers to sound the cymbals as the Ark was brought back to the Holy City (1 Chronicles 15:16-19). Apparently Asaph did his job well because when the Ark was safely back in place, King David appointed Asaph as his chief minister to celebrate, thank and praise the Lord (1 Chronicles 16:5). His primary responsibility was "to minister before the ark continually, as every day's work required" (1 Chronicles 16:37).

Many Bible scholars believe Asaph also headed up a music school for as many as 148 students. Asaph was a talented fellow, a great musician with a desire to please God. He was a skilled motivator who knew how to bring out the best from others, and he could inspire people to great heights.

His style was distinctive and forceful, yet deeply sensitive. He is referred to in the Bible as both a prophet (2 Chronicles 21:30) and a singer (Nehemiah 12:46)—a noble distinction, indeed.

But when you study Psalm 73, you soon discover that

Asaph is discouraged; he is depressed. He is a frustrated musician who just can't understand what in the world God is doing.

Asaph's question was: "How can an all-powerful, holy, good God allow the wicked to prosper while the righteous folks go unrewarded?" Have you ever wondered about that? Why do good things happen to bad people?

As a young minister fresh out of college, I worked for a while with a famous evangelist who I knew (but couldn't prove) was having an affair with his secretary. The preacher explained he needed his secretary to travel with him on out-of-town trips, for business reasons of course, but her husband always had to work in the ministry offices back home.

Even in town, the evangelist's motives and actions were often suspect. I vividly recall visiting him at his office and staring in shock and dismay as the evangelist caressed a glass of wine with one hand and his secretary with the other.

Strangely, the man and his ministry continued to prosper. He was respected and honored among his peers. Had he not chosen to pursue another vocation, he might still be making the rounds on his circuit.

I was confused. I said, "God, this doesn't make any sense to me. You know that guy isn't living right. He's making a mockery of You and me both. Why are you letting him get away with it? And prospering yet? God, it just isn't fair!"

Asaph must have felt something like that. And Asaph's feelings were further complicated by the fact that the Hebrews believed that material prosperity was the best way to measure spiritual blessings—a time quite similar to our own.

Asaph had a problem. He had believed God for good

things, but the blessings were not coming, at least, not according to Asaph's agenda. Consequently, Asaph began to question: "God? Why? Why are You withholding Your blessings from me while known pagans are prospering? I've kept the rules. I have been trying with all my heart to live for You and to love You. I've loved the things You love, and hated the things You hate.

"Why then, Lord, do those people who don't even pretend to love You seem to be getting so far ahead in life? I thought *we* were Your special children. Yet people who don't care a bit about You are blessed. Everything keeps going their way!"

Have you ever felt this way?

"God, I'm trying to do right and live by Your Word. But I'm miserable, and my non-Christian buddies are still having a good time."

"I'm striving to operate my business according to Your standards; we even close on the Sabbath. But our competitors are bowling us over."

"My social life is pure and I've refused to compromise my moral values. So why am I the one sitting home alone all the time?"

"We really do desire to tithe our family income and to put the Lord first in every area, but we're struggling to survive. Meanwhile, those folks down the street, who don't even care about You, are doing just great. God, it's not fair!"

"Lord, You know that girl cheated on the test and got an *A.* I studied hard, did my own work and got a *C!*"

"That guy who connives and manipulates at work got a raise! I've been working there longer than he has and I haven't had a promotion since I started!"

"What about that guy who takes huge, unmerited

deductions on his income tax, shading the truth and shuffling the figures? The Internal Revenue Service sent him a $1200 refund check! What did I get? *Audited!*"

These are some of the contemporary refrains of the "Sad Song of Asaph." The unspoken common denominator of these disheartened laments is: "God, I trusted You, and it seems to me that the bottom line ought to be better."

That's how Asaph felt. He believed in his heart that God is good to His people, especially to those who are pure in heart (Psalm 73:1). But then he admits, "As for me, my feet came close to stumbling; my steps had almost slipped" (Psalm 73:2).

The Futility and Foolishness of Human Comparisons

Fortunately for us, Asaph was honest enough to reveal the cause of his discontent. He traced the beginning of his problems to his own foolish, negative attitude: "For I was envious of the arrogant" (Psalm 73:3).

One Christian woman confessed, "It's not that I envy my affluent neighbors; I envy my neighbors' *things.*"

So did Asaph. He saw the prosperity of the wicked, their relative ease and their freedom from personal pain, and it bothered him (Psalm 73:3-5). Furthermore, their physical health and apparent exemption from calamity caused these wicked people to become all the more arrogant, boastful and proud. Asaph notes: "Pride is their necklace" (Psalm 73:6).

Did Asaph have a good gripe? You know he did! These people were insolent and insensitive. Their actions and attitudes were gross, haughty, ignorant and insulting. They even dared to blaspheme God (Psalm 73:9-12). They flagrantly defied God with their cynical disrespect. They taunted: "How does God know? And is there knowledge with the Most High?" (Psalm 73:11)

Because God had not snuffed them out in judgment, these wicked ones were assuming that either God did not know what they were doing, that He didn't care, or that He wouldn't or couldn't do anything about their sinful conduct.

The skepticism and cynicism of sinful society should not surprise us. The apostle Paul warns:

> Walk no longer just as the Gentiles also walk, in the futility of their mind, being darkened in their under-standing, excluded from the life of God, because of the ignorance that is in them, because of the hardness of their heart; and they, having become callous, have given themselves over to sensuality, for the practice of every kind of impurity with greediness. *But you did not learn Christ in this way*, if indeed you have heard Him (Ephesians 4:17-21, italics mine).

Paul is saying, "Of course, you can expect sinful behavior from sinful society, but *you* are supposed to be counterculture. Stop comparing yourself to the people of the world. You are to have *different* attitudes because you serve a different God!"

At this point, though, it is too easy to identify with Asaph. What's the use in being good if the righteous go unrewarded and the pagans go unpunished?

> Surely in vain I have kept my heart pure, and washed my hands in innocence; for I have been stricken all day long, and chastened every morning (Psalm 73:13,14).

Certainly, Asaph's estimation of the situation is exag-gerated. Bad things do happen to bad people, just as surely as good things come to good people. Regardless, Asaph's complaint seemed valid, and to him that's all that mattered.

Sometimes, well intentioned friends will attempt to console you by saying, "Well, you shouldn't *feel* that way." Whereupon, you want to punch them while you shout, "But I *do* feel that way!" Still, wallowing in the futility and falseness of human comparisons will only stifle future blessings. You must get out of that pit, but how?

Pulling Out of the Pits of Self-Pity

What can you do to overcome the disillusionment that comes with Asaph's song? First, start by changing your own attitude.

An attitude change normally requires an act of your will. You consciously decide you are going to respond positively to your situation. Sounds simple, right? You know better. Sometimes you find that you are unable to change your inner feelings on your own. Said one honest fellow, "If I could change my own attitude, do you think I'd keep the one I've got?" When you find yourself lacking the power to change your attitude, that's the time to call out to the Lord for help.

Frequently you will find that confession of sin is involved. If so, admit any sinful attitudes or actions that you have been harboring. Keep in mind that envy, lust or jealousy are serious sins capable of destroying your relationship with God. Repent and allow the Lord to cleanse your heart, to forgive you and, yes, to change your attitude. The apostle Paul says, "Have this attitude in yourselves which was also in Christ Jesus" (Philippians 2:5).

Asaph acknowledged what his bad attitude was doing to him (Psalm 73:15,16). Even beyond that, he realized his negative thinking might prove potentially destructive in the minds of others in God's family. He said, "If I had said, 'I will speak this,' behold I should have betrayed the generation of thy children" (Psalm 73:15). As disgruntled as Asaph was, he knew enough to keep his mouth shut rather than to hurt others with his words, especially impressionable younger believers.

What about your attitude? What kind of impact is it having upon those younger believers who may be looking to you as an example of spiritual maturity?

After a squabble among his spiritual leaders, I overheard one astute teenager say, "Whew! *That's* supposed to be a saint? That's what I'm supposed to aspire to? No way!"

Jesus said, "Whoever causes one of these little ones who believe in Me to stumble, it is better for him that a heavy millstone be hung around his neck, and that he be drowned in the depth of the sea" (Matthew 18:6). Granted, Jesus was speaking specifically about causing the children to stumble, but the warning was clear to anyone who would become a stumbling block to somebody else.

Asaph must have understood this, for he says:

> When I pondered to understand this, it was troublesome in my sight until I came into the sanctuary of God; then I perceived their end (Psalm 73:16,17).

We've reached the turning point in Asaph's attitude: He entered the sanctuary of God. Wait a minute! Asaph was a priest and a professional minister of music. He was in "church" nearly every day of his life. What was so special about this trip to the sanctuary?

Millions of disillusioned Christians sit in services every week only to find that the church is long on form and formulas but pathetically short on answers that satisfy a hungry soul. To tell a disillusioned Christian that the answer to his or her problem is to go to church is like pouring water on a drowning man.

Obviously, Asaph was not talking about merely going into the church building again.

The "sanctuary" of which Asaph speaks was the place

where God's presence was made known to man. Asaph came not to a building, but to the builder; not simply to a place where God's people gathered occasionally, but right into the presence of God Himself. Asaph discovered the person of God, not merely more information about Him. What a difference!

When he entered God's presence, Asaph *perceived* the answer to his questions. Significantly, his mind was affected in the presence of God, not simply his emotions or his feelings. Author Malcolm Smith comments:

> The spiritually exhausted person needs more than the singing of a few inspirational worship songs—they will only momentarily make him feel good. He needs a completely new perspective on the way he thinks about life. When that happens, the inspiration will last a lifetime.[1]

When your mind is illumined by the Spirit of God, you will find that the seeming successes of sinful people no longer upset you. In fact, you may be saddened as you perceive their end. They are hurtling headlong toward destruction. Rather than feeling anger and resentment over their material prosperity, your heart may break over their spiritual poverty.

As Asaph came into God's presence, he began to understand the difference between the transient and the eternal. He realized that God's final judgments were still to come, and when they did, the wicked would be found wanting. Asaph may have gasped as he said:

> Surely Thou dost set them in slippery places; Thou dost cast them down to destruction. How they are destroyed in a moment! They are utterly swept away by sudden terrors! (Psalm 73:18,19)

Perhaps Asaph understood in a fresh way that the ultimate purpose of this life is not simply to grab all the gusto you can, but to get ready for an eternal existence. Viewing life from this perspective totally transformed his attitude.

Moreover, when he looked back upon his mistake, he admitted he was irritated with God and bitter toward other people. He says, "I was senseless and ignorant . . . like a beast before Thee" (Psalm 73:22). Asaph's comparison is apt; a wild beast acts only according to the information provided by its senses. Similarly, Asaph's disillusionment came whenever he acted upon what he saw and heard, rather than from his relationship with, and knowledge of, Almighty God. Have you seen any "beastly" Christians lately in church? At home? In the mirror?

As Asaph considered how close he came to personal destruction, he expresses his awe that through it all, God had never left him. And then Asaph begins to praise God (Psalm 73:22-28). An important principle is modeled here: True praise comes after the heart is cleansed, not before. Isn't that astounding? Remember, Asaph was the leading praise and worship leader in the land. He was the fellow who had the responsibility of teaching everyone else how to enter into the praise and worship of the Lord.

But he was helpless to do so until he allowed God to cleanse *his* heart of impure attitudes. Only then was Asaph able to minister in the freedom of God's presence; only then did he understand what praise and worship is all about; only then did Asaph see the true meaning of *success*.

9

God Loves
Losers, Too!

In one area after another, Christians are adopting the world's ideas of what it means to be a winner.

Society places an enormous amount of pressure on an individual to succeed. Get the good job. Make the best grades. Play first chair in the orchestra. Earn more and more money. Win the big game.

Rarely do you see an athlete on television running toward the camera with two fingers pointed in the air as he shouts, "We're Number Two! We're Number Two!" Being Number One is what life is all about.

At least, that's what we are taught.

Recently, I was thumbing through a magazine which boldly boasted, "The 50 Most Beautiful People in the World." As I glanced through their choices, I thought, *If this is what it means to be a beautiful person, I'm in big trouble!* Most of the selections were Hollywood stars, great athletes or famous musicians; nary a preacher among them. Nobody like me made the list.

When I get up in the morning, I look in the mirror (as soon as I work up the courage), and I *know* that God has a sense of humor. I got the feeling from reading the magazine that most of the beautiful people get up in the morning, look in the mirror and start singing, "How Great Thou Art."

Most Christians would say, "Aw, that's just Hollywood. That's 'worldly' success." True. Unfortunately, the church has been duped into adopting many of sinful society's concepts of success.

That's why it is vitally important that you understand: *God loves losers, too!*

The "Christian" Measuring Stick

Christians have the annoying habit of using worldly standards and superficial measuring sticks to determine levels of success and the value of a person. This is a common plague among pastors. Multitudes of good, godly pastors feel like failures although they have been faithfully serving the Lord and their congregations. When they hear of a church down the road, or in the next state, or around the world, that has thousands of members, the pastor of the small, local church begins wringing his hands and wondering, *What am I doing wrong?*

I've discovered superficial measuring sticks among Christian speakers. To some, the big issue has little to do with people hearing about Jesus; it's the bottom line that counts: "Sure, you want to point people to Jesus, but tell me the truth. How much money are you making?"

Some people truly *are* interested in spiritual success more than temporal, monetary success . . . at first. But after a while, they begin to apply the same warped, worldly measuring rods to determine the value of spiritual victories: "How many souls have you won to Christ today? Ten? Twenty? How many did you convert last week? This month? This past year? One hundred? Five hundred? A thousand?" In the quest for ever-increasing numbers, many men and women of God seem to have forgotten that the angels in heaven rejoice over *one* person who is saved from hell and brought into the kingdom of God.

The same subtle, worldly success syndrome can be seen in the fight against abortion in America. The success-oriented Christian may hear about a pro-life demonstration in which the participants are rejoicing, "We helped prevent three abortions today! Hallelujah!"

Three abortions? the success-oriented Christian thinks. *What's the big deal? Thousands of other legalized murders will take place somewhere else today. Why are you making such a fuss over three children? Call me when you prevent one thousand abortions, or three thousand, or three million.*

What the success-oriented Christian fails to realize is that three human babies *will* be born. They now have an opportunity to make a difference that will affect eternity. Those Christians who do not appreciate the value of the individual person are the ones who refuse to get involved unless you are talking about "mega-ministry."

In one area after another, Christians are adopting the world's ideas of what it means to be a winner. Yet even more alarming, we have allowed these false, warped values to color, confound and confuse what it means to be a success in our personal spiritual adventures.

Working So Hard to Be Christian

Multitudes of modern believers feel like abject failures in their spiritual lives. Why?

Because they don't love Jesus?

No.

Because they have not repented of their sins?

No.

Because the Lord has not forgiven them and washed

their hearts and minds whiter than snow?

No.

Why, then?

Because while desperately desiring to be successful in their lives, they have been sucked into the snare of measuring their progress by worldly standards. They insist upon comparing themselves to everybody else. They try to measure up on their own effort or merit. They are trying to be "good" under their own power. Frustration soon follows when these sincere believers realize they have failed . . . again.

A strong, burly football player approached me after I had spoken to his team. His commitment to Christ was genuine, but his understanding of how the Christian life functions was seriously deficient. He declared confidently, "I want to be a *good* Christian. No, no, no. I want to be a *great* Christian and I'm going to keep working at this thing harder and harder until I get it right!"

He was too big for me to argue with, so I gave him my phone number and told him to call me when he gets trapped in his own end zone.

That football player is a product of our contemporary "Positive Christianity." Many pastors refuse to preach anything but uplifting, motivational messages. Author and evangelist David Wilkerson notes:

> To hear them tell it, every Christian is receiving miracles; everybody is getting instant answers to prayer; everybody is feeling good, living good, and the whole world is bright and rosy. I love to hear that kind of preaching, because I really desire all those good and healthy things for God's people. But that's not the way things are for a great number of very honest, sincere Christians. How sad to hear such shallow theology being pushed from pulpits today. . . . It is this kind of materialistic preaching that has so ill prepared an entire

generation to endure any kind of pain, to be content with such things as they have, to be abased and not always abounding. Serving God becomes a kind of Olympic race, in which everyone must strive for the gold medals.[1]

The False Path of Personal Perfectionism

How important it is for us to recall the word that God gave to the prophet Zechariah: "'Not by might nor by power, but by My Spirit,' says the Lord of hosts" (Zechariah 4:6). God told His prophet that His Temple would be built, His mighty work would get done, but it would not be because of sheer human effort. It would have a supernatural touch upon it.

The same touch is needed in your life, if you are ever to overcome your spiritual impotence. Try as you might with your own strength, but you will never perfectly please the Lord. At this point, many Christians give up in despair and become depressed, discouraged or disillusioned. Some drop out of fellowship completely.

The devil has defeated these Christians through one of his most devious devices: He has deceived them into pursuing a false path of personal perfectionism. Operating under their own power, comparing their success or lack of success with artificially imposed standards of perfection, they are on a perpetual treadmill, traveling the road to nowhere except fatigue, discouragement and exhaustion.

"Wait a minute!" you may be saying. "Doesn't Jesus tell us that we *should* be perfect, even as our Father in heaven is perfect?"

Yes, He does, and I believe He means exactly what He said. Understand, though, that there is literally a world of difference between the Holy Spirit making you perfect through His power and you striving toward perfection under your own power. As the Holy Spirit fills our lives, He makes us holy people and whole people. On the other hand, that devilish, worldly, counterfeit perfectionism destroys our peace with God, causes us to become spiritual Pharisees, leads us into emotional bondage and creates such strain in our lives that we feel we are coming apart at the seams.

The Holy Spirit's perfect work causes your life to become *integrated*; the disillusioning, success-driven, pseudo-perfection causes your life to *disintegrate*. You will never be able to do enough or be "good" enough to please and be accepted by the god you have created in your own mind.

John Fletcher, an eighteenth century preacher, noticed this creeping perfectionism in his congregation. His two-hundred-year-old comments may sound as though he is describing the members of your church:

> Some of them bind heavy burdens on themselves of their own making and when they cannot bear them, they are tormented in their consciences with imaginary guilt.
>
> Others go around with constant fear of having committed the unpardonable sin. . . . We're seeing all sorts of people who ought to be happy and content in their spiritual lives, but who feel like terrible sinners, and that there is no hope for them whatsoever.[2]

Does his assessment sound familiar to you? Fletcher goes on to record John Wesley's thoughts on the matter:

> Sometimes this excellent quality, tenderness of conscience, is carried to an extreme. We find some [Christians] who fear where no fear is, who are continually condemning themselves without cause, imagining something to be sinful where Scripture nowhere condemns it, supposing other things to be their duty where Scripture nowhere enjoins it. This . . . is a sore evil. It is highly expedient to yield to it as little as possible, rather it is a matter of prayer that you may be delivered from this sore evil and may recover a sound mind.[3]

Ironically, John Wesley is the fellow who wrote the book on Christian "perfection." His often misunderstood work, *A Plain Account of Christian Perfection,* is a classic.

Understand, neither Fletcher nor Wesley were encouraging Christians to be lazy in their spiritual lives or tolerant of willful sin. These preachers were not wild-eyed-pinko-communist-humanistic-liberals. They were two of the most conservative preachers and theologians of their day (and ours).

Both preached repentance of sins, holiness of lifestyle, dedication, devotion and discipline. As a member of what we would now call an accountability group, known then as "The Holy Club," Wesley's personal commitment to methodical spiritual disciplines was well known. When his followers later broke with the organized Church of England, it was only natural to refer to them as "Methodists."

Nevertheless, Wesley was saying, "You are thinking that you are doing terribly in your spiritual life and *you are not!* Yet you continue to beat up yourself because you are not a spiritual success, strapping yourself with one yoke of bondage after another."

Jesus says:

Come to Me, all who are weary and heavy-laden, and I will give you rest. Take My yoke upon you, and learn from Me, for I am gentle and humble in heart; and YOU SHALL FIND REST FOR YOUR SOULS. For My yoke is easy, and My load is light (Matthew 11:28-30).

Jesus said that He would give you *rest*—not a heavier load of guilt and condemnation; not a dozen more things to do before He will accept you. That's good news if you are weak, weary, burdened down, burned out, whipped or worn.

Jesus loves losers, too! He doesn't say, "Keep striving

and you might make it." He says, "Relax. Rest. Come to Me. My Yoke is easy and My load is light." What a far cry this is from the perfectionist's thinking.

Symptoms of a Perfectionist

To the perfectionist, nothing is ever quite good enough. It is never completely right. He or she lives with the attitude, "Well, that's okay, but I could have done it better."

What are some signs that you may be, or may be becoming, a perfectionist? Four stand out to me.

1. You are never pleased with yourself.

In *Healing for Damaged Emotions,* author David Seamands writes that perfectionists live with the "tyranny of the oughts." It sounds like this:

"I ought to have done this or that."

"I ought to have done better."

"I got a *B* on that last test, but I ought to have been able to get an *A*."

"I read three chapters of the Bible today. I should have read five."

"I witnessed to two people about Jesus this week. I should have witnessed to ten."

"I made $25,000 last year. I should have been able to make $35,000."

"I took care of the kids, got the family's supper and gave the children their baths. If only I had worked harder, I could have washed the dishes, done the vacuuming and dusted the furniture."

Connie, a Christian woman in her mid-fifties, has the cleanest house I've ever seen . . . and is one of the loneliest people I've ever met. She is a "clean-a-holic." She picks up the spoon before you're done stirring your coffee. The dust doesn't settle on the windowsill before she comes along with a damp cloth. You probably could safely eat off her floors. The woman is obsessed with keeping her house clean.

Unfortunately, in her quest for the perfectly clean house, she has driven her friends and family members right out of it. Perfectionists aren't much fun to be around for long.

2. It seems as though God is never really pleased with you.

You feel like God is always saying, "Come on, now. You know you can do better than that."

Steve, a rugged, hardworking carpenter, told me, "It's like I work so hard to climb up the ladder toward God. Then, just about the time I near the top, God pulls the ladder up a little higher!"

Since perfectionists incessantly feel that they didn't do enough or they didn't do what they did well enough, God is never truly happy with their progress. Three phrases dominate the perfectionist's prayer life: I *could* have; I *should* have; I *would* have. The perfectionist is always striving but never arriving.

While it is noble to want to do more for God, to serve Him more fully or to dedicate oneself more completely, it is absolutely impossible to *work* yourself into His favor. God doesn't give brownie points.

3. Your life is filled with constant anxiety.

Spiritual anxiety may manifest itself in the form of tension, worry, fear, anger, discontent or condemnation. It is that awful feeling of, "I wonder if God is mad at me. No, I *know* God is mad at me!" You pray and repent of the same sins that you confessed hundreds of times before. You feel slightly better, but nothing has fundamentally changed. You stay spiritually strong for a few days, then fall right back into the ruts:

> "I can't get this Christian life right!"
>
> "God must really hate me now."
>
> "I'm never going to 'get the victory.' "

All of this, of course, causes you to be even more disconsolate concerning your spiritual life. When this happens, the spiritual perfectionist frequently develops a fourth symptom.

4. Your life is controlled by legalism.

It may seem odd that the natural progression of perfectionism is toward establishing a list of "do's" and "don'ts," but think about it. The spiritual perfectionist is never quite pleased with himself or herself. He is never sure that God is pleased. He lives with constant anxiety and inner turmoil. Consequently, it becomes even more imperative in the perfectionist's mind that he *look* and *sound* spiritual to everybody else.

The easiest way to do that is to squawk a lot about what you *do* or *don't do* in the name of the Lord. "I don't drink; I don't smoke; I don't chew tobacco; I don't watch dirty movies; I don't go to dances. I do read twenty chapters of the Bible and pray for two hours every day. I fast at least two days per week. I memorized Psalm 119. I was here for the six o'clock morning prayer meeting. Where were *you?*"

The perfectionist thinks, "Maybe if I give up this bad habit, God will accept me. Maybe if I quit doing that and start doing this, quit going there and start going here, God will be pleased with me. Maybe then I can make God happy." Meanwhile, the impossible list of do's and don'ts keeps growing longer, and more people must be pleased or impressed to keep up the act. Before long, the spiritual perfectionist, who started out with the desire to please God and be a good Christian, now hates or fears God and is saddled with what the apostle Paul called a "yoke of bondage."

Wearing Our Yokes

Strange, isn't it, how Christians will create yokes of bondage for themselves and for others? Those yokes are not easy, nor are they light. Those yokes are heavy. They are killers.

The Bible refers to a yoke in two ways. First, it speaks of "yoking together," as in the linking together of two animals to plow a field.

Second, the yoke was a symbol of overbearing, tyrannical authority. It was the word used to describe the despotic burdens laid upon the necks of a conquered, broken people as the symbol of their slavery. The yoke symbolized humiliation and despair.

But the good news is that Jesus Christ has broken the yoke of slavery and bondage. By His blood on Calvary's cross, Christ conquered the conquerors, shattering the yoke of sin once and for all. He broke down every barrier between you and God and made a way for you to be forgiven and accepted. He even sent His Spirit to live within you, empowering you to live in a manner that is pleasing to God!

Although you can never *earn* God's approval or *win* God's favor, you can have both by trusting in Christ freely. While you can never work hard enough to merit the honor of His presence, He freely opens the door and allows you to enter. You are brought into His presence not on the basis of your success, but on the basis of your relationship through Jesus Christ. Perhaps that is why Paul wrote, "For by grace you have been saved through faith; and that not of yourselves, it is the gift of God; not as a result of works, that no one should boast" (Ephesians 2:8,9).

Grace is a free gift, something that is unearned and undeserved. I doubt we will ever truly understand it. All we can do is humble ourselves and graciously accept it, thanking the Lord for setting us free. Disillusionment no longer has a foothold because all illusions of "succeeding" as a Christian have been replaced with a realistic appraisal of oneself and a "gratitude attitude" toward our heavenly Father's gift of salvation and the Holy Spirit's accomplishments in and through us.

Curing the Spiritual Success Syndrome

If your struggle with the spiritual success syndrome has resulted in disillusionment, remember these four simple truths:

1. *Jesus really does love you unconditionally.* Nothing you can do will ever earn that love, and nothing you have done or will ever do can destroy that love. You can't "unearn" what you never earned in the first place.

2. *Jesus really forgives you.* If you have honestly repented, which means to turn around and turn away from your sin, you are forgiven. The Bible says, "There is therefore now no condemnation for those who are in Christ Jesus" (Romans 8:1).

3. *Jesus really accepts you, just the way you are.* One fellow told me, "I've sung that old hymn, 'Just As I Am' hundreds of times, but I never caught the message. Whenever I'd pray, I always pretended that I was a better guy than I knew I was. Lately, I haven't been doing that. I've been coming to Him and saying, 'Lord, it's me; and I've messed up again.' You know, being honest with God has done wonders for my spiritual life!"

God knows where you are and what you are going through. You needn't paint a pretty picture for Him. He accepts you. If others don't, that's their problem.

4. *Jesus really is pleased with your progress so far.* Certainly, you want to press on. You are still growing, and you are still in the building process. But understand, the

renovation has begun!

The great English writer C. S. Lewis knew well the temptations to judge ourselves and each other by false standards. He also understood the balance between our perseverance and God's patience with our imperfections:

> On the one hand, God's demand for perfection need not discourage you in the least in your present attempts to be good, or even in your present failures. Each time you fall He will pick you up again. And He knows perfectly well that your own efforts are never going to bring you anywhere near perfection. On the other hand, you must realize from the outset that the goal toward which He is beginning to guide you is absolute perfection; and no power in the whole universe, except you yourself, can prevent Him from taking you to the goal.[4]

Borrowing from George MacDonald, another great writer, Lewis continued:

> Imagine yourself as a living house. God comes in to rebuild that house. At first, perhaps, you can understand what He is doing. He is getting the drains right and stopping the leaks in the roof and so on; you knew that those jobs needed doing and so you are not surprised. But presently He starts knocking the house about in a way that hurts abominably and does not seem to make sense.
>
> What on earth is He up to? The explanation is that He is building quite a different house from the one you thought of. . . . You thought you were going to be made into a decent little cottage: but He is building a palace. He intends to come and live in it himself.[5]

If you think that you don't deserve God's grace, you are right. But then again, neither do the rest of us. And neither did a fellow in the Bible whose disillusionment almost cost him a seat at the king's table . . .

10

Defective Concepts of Christianity

The King does not want to destroy you;
He wants to save and restore you!

The war was finally over. King David had succeeded in defeating the Philistines, Israel's perennial enemy, and quelling all opposition at home. In the process, David had expanded the borders of his country, built a strong force of mighty warriors, and brought respect and prosperity back to his nation. It was a great time in Israel's history.

Perhaps David was in a mellow mood. Or maybe now that he was free from the pressures and crisis management on the battlefront, he could afford to mull over the tumultuous events of his life. For whatever reason, David's thoughts turned toward his best friend, Jonathan, who had died in battle along with his father, Saul.

The king asked his aides, "Is there yet anyone left of the house of Saul, that I may show him kindness for Jonathan's sake?" (2 Samuel 9:1) David was recalling his deep relationship with Jonathan. Years before, David and Jonathan had entered into a covenant relationship in which they had promised to protect, defend and preserve each other, no matter what.

Jonathan had initiated the covenant while his father was the reigning monarch in Israel (1 Samuel 18:3,4). Later, when both Jonathan and David were beginning to sense Saul's ominous nature and his attitude toward David, they reiterated their commitment to each other. And though Jonathan was the king's son and, by all human standards, in line for Saul's throne, it almost sounds as though he has a premonition about his future:

> "May the LORD be with you as He has been with my father. And if I am still alive, will you not show me the lovingkindness of the Lord, that I may not die? And you shall not cut off your lovingkindness from my house forever, not even when the Lord cuts off every one of the enemies of David from the face of the earth." So Jonathan made a covenant with the house of David, saying, "May the LORD require it at the hands of David's enemies." And Jonathan made David vow again because of his love for him, because he loved him as he loved his own life (1 Samuel 20:13-17).

This was a serious promise between these two young men. Many Bible scholars believe that it was not merely a "love" covenant; it was also a *blood* covenant.

As a youngster I loved to watch cowboys and Indians on television. I was intrigued when the leader of the "pale faces" and the leader of the "In-juns" slowly and ritualistically cut each other's palms with a knife and then rubbed their hands together, mixing the blood. They became "blood brothers." Although I never quite understood the ramifications, I knew that the wild west was a safer place to be because of their intimate relationship.

More Than A Promise

Actually, the westerns' portrayal of the blood covenant was very similar to the blood covenant in Old Testament times. First, the two parties would take off their coats and exchange them. When Jonathan and David did this (1 Samuel 18:4), they were saying to each other, "All that I am, everything I have, is now available to you."

Next, the two would exchange their weapons, if they had any, including bows, swords and shields of armor (18:4). By this they were saying to each other, "All of my power is available to you. If you ever need help or protection, I'll be there for you."

This was followed by the actual cutting of the palms and the clasping together of the hands. Our modern custom of shaking hands may have its origins in this ancient Hebrew rite.

Then, rather than simply wiping their hands clean and bandaging their wounds, the wounds were sealed shut in a manner certain to leave a scar. That scar was an obvious, tangible, visible witness that this person was bound in a covenant relationship with another person. Our modern practice of wearing a wedding ring is meant to symbolize something similar.

After the cutting of the palms and the sealing of the wounds, the parties would then announce the blessings and the curses associated with the pact. Most had the general tenor of: "If you keep the covenant, you will be blessed. If you do not keep your promise, these curses will come upon you."

Following the announcement, the participants ate a symbolic meal together, often consisting simply of bread and wine. During the meal, they stated their promises once again and reminded each other, as did Jonathan and David, that this covenant was binding on their family members and future descendants.

This was the relationship into which David and Jonathan had entered.

Thus, when David mused over the possibilities of doing something nice for Jonathan's descendants, he was not merely feeling magnanimous. He felt duty-bound.

David's aides soon discovered a way to help fulfill their king's desire:

> Now there was a servant of the house of Saul whose name was Ziba, and they called him to David; and the king said to him, "Are you Ziba?" And he said, "I am your servant." And the king said, "Is there not yet anyone of the house of Saul to whom I may show the kindness of God?" And Ziba said to the king, "There is still a son of Jonathan who is crippled in both feet" (2 Samuel 9:2,3).

Is it just me, or do you get the impression from this passage that Ziba was not exactly thrilled to be providing information to King David? After all, Ziba was of the house of Saul, and Saul was suspicious and jealous of David until the day he drew his last breath and fell on his own sword. Ziba wouldn't dare lie to the king, but maybe he was attempting to divert David's attention away from Jonathan's son by the manner in which he volunteered, "Well, there is one son, but he's crippled in both feet."

David could not be deflected. "Where is he?" he wanted to know.

"In Lo-debar," Ziba answered.

Down and Out in the Wilderness

Mephibosheth was the crippled man's name. Years before, when Mephibosheth was only five years old, his family heard the awful news that Saul and Jonathan had fallen on the battlefield. It was obvious to almost everyone that David was the Lord's choice as Saul's successor. Consequently, the remaining members of Saul's family fled for their lives. In the Middle East, when a monarch of one ruling family died and another family ascended the throne, the normal policy was to exterminate any remaining heirs from the previous family.

Saul's family may have felt that David would treat them poorly, so they fled in panic. In their haste, Mephibosheth's nurse "took him up and fled. And it happened that in her hurry to flee, he fell and became lame" (2 Samuel 4:4).

They took young Mephibosheth as far away as they could, into the wilderness to a desolate place, a place nobody wanted to visit. The place of *Lo-debar*. The name itself means "a barren place" and that's what it was. Lo-debar was not exactly a vacation paradise. It was a dump. But it was a place of hiding and, hopefully, safety.

The Bible gives no information about Mephibosheth's youth, but can you imagine what was driven into that young boy's brain during those years in barren Lo-debar? Do you suppose he heard what a great man of God King David was? Or how David and his dad had been such close buddies? Or how Saul had slain his thousands but David had slain his ten thousands?

I doubt it. Human nature being what it is, most likely Saul's household drove their bitterness into little Mephibosheth's heart and mind.

"You've been done dirty, boy!"

"That's right, son. You are the one who should be king, not that David fellow. And to think, after all your dad did for him . . . "

"You're the king's kid! Why, your grandfather was the first king of Israel. You ought to be in the palace. You should be on the throne!"

"And if we wouldn't have had to flee for our lives, you wouldn't be crippled today. It's all David's fault."

No doubt Mephibosheth had a warped image of the king. As he dragged his feet through the wilderness sand, leaning on his homemade crutches, I imagine

Mephibosheth cringed at the very name of David.

Then one day, a messenger came: "King David wants to see you, and I'm here to take you to him."

What do you suppose went through Mephibosheth's mind? Again the Scripture is silent, but I can imagine the young man, in his early twenties now, reeling in horror. "Oh, no! He's found me! After all these years of hiding from him and avoiding any contact with his representatives, he's finally caught me. It's over. I'm a dead man."

From the Desert to the Palace

But that was not the reason King David was seeking this poor, crippled desert-dweller. Mephibosheth didn't know it, but the king didn't want to kill him; he wanted to bless him!

If you have been living with hatred, jealousy, fear, animosity and bitterness out in the wilderness of spiritual dryness and disillusionment, please receive this message: The King does not want to *destroy* you; He wants to save and restore you! He wants to bring you back into His presence, to give you a new start, another chance at life.

Don't run from Him; run to Him!

Undoubtedly, Mephibosheth's crippled legs were quaking when the messenger brought him to King David. He fell on his face before the king, partly out of respect, partly from fright. After all, this may have been the first time he had ever really *seen* this awesome king about whom he had heard so much. Now here he was in the king's presence! And as an enemy of the king.

David's words must have stunned Mephibosheth. The king said, "Do not fear."

The excellent preacher and author Charles Swindoll sees Christ-like grace in David's exhortation. In his book *The Grace Awakening*, Swindoll asks:

Do you know what was the most oft-repeated command from [Jesus'] lips? Most people I ask are unable to answer that question correctly. Our Lord issued numerous commands, but He made this one more than any other. Do you happen to know what it was? It was this: "Fear not." *Isn't that great?* "Do not fear." Naturally, the most common reaction when someone stood before the perfect Son of God would have been fear. And yet Jesus, great in grace, repeatedly said, "Do not be afraid."

He didn't meet people with a deep frown, looking down on them and swinging a club. He met them with open arms and reassuring words, "Don't be afraid." Those are the words David used before Mephibosheth. They drip with grace.[1]

David went on to say, "I will surely show kindness to you for the sake of your father Jonathan" (2 Samuel 9:7).

The unspoken message of David's words was, "I don't want to hurt you; I want to bless you. Although this is a new kingdom, and you are legally under a death sentence, I want you to live like a king's kid. I want you to eat at the king's table. I am going to restore to you all that was taken from you in the fall and a whole lot more! I am doing these things not because of anything *you* have done and not because you deserve it, but because I have a covenant with Jonathan. Upon the basis of that covenant, you can come boldly into my house and make yourself at home!"

Mephibosheth's reply is classic: "What is your servant, that you should regard a dead dog like me?" (2 Samuel 9:8)

Talk about a poor self-image! Mephibosheth couldn't believe that something this fabulous could be happening to him. By calling himself a dead dog, he was groveling as low as he could go, "Surely, Great King, that is too good to be true for a low-life like me."

But David was emphatic.

Then the king called Ziba and said to him:

> All that belonged to Saul and to all his house I have
> given to your master's grandson. And you and your sons
> and your servants shall cultivate the land for him, and
> you shall bring in the produce so that your master's
> grandson may have food; nevertheless Mephi-
> bosheth your master's grandson shall eat at my table regularly (2
> Samuel 9:10).

Don't you wish you could have seen the look on Ziba's
face? The man who just a short time ago had spoken almost
sarcastically about his master's son was now Mephibosheth's servant.

Better still, can you imagine what the religious crowd
in town said when they heard that Mephibosheth was eating
regularly at David's table? No doubt their unsanctified
memories served them too well:

"What's that grandson of Saul doing eating at David's
table?"

"Why, remember all the trouble that Saul gave David?
That's Jonathan's kid; he's got gall."

"Yes, and after all the things those dust-balls out in
Lo-debar said about David. Look at that Mephibosheth right
in there with the king. Who does he think he is?"

Quite possibly Mephibosheth himself may have had
misgivings about imposing on the king's kindness. Maybe
he thought, *I don't deserve this. What am I doing here?
After all I have said? The things I have thought! My
attitude and actions were terrible!*

But Mephibosheth's relationship with David was not
based upon his worth in any way. It was established by the
covenant between David and Jonathan.

In my imagination I can see David's royal family and
top advisors around the dinner table: Solomon, Absalom,
Amnon, Joab and others. And oh, yes, there's

Mephibosheth. Looking around that room, Mephibosheth could easily be haunted by feelings of inferiority. Then, in my mind's eye, I see David pass a plate to Mephibosheth, and when he does, his upturned palm is at precisely the correct angle for Mephibosheth to see the scar—the permanent reminder of David's loving covenant with Jonathan. And Mephibosheth can breathe easy as he recalls, "Yes, the blood covenant; that's why I am here."

One of these days in heaven, you may wonder, "What in the world am I doing here? I surely don't deserve *this* after the things I've said, thought and done."

Then you will look and see the nail-scarred hands of Jesus, and you will remember that it was not your goodness that got you into heaven. It was because of His blood. Because of that, the king says, "Come and eat at My table."

What Did I Do to Deserve This?

What does all this have to do with being a disillusioned Christian? Simply this: Until you understand that your relationship with God is a blood-covenant relationship, you will be trapped in a performance-oriented, defective concept of Christianity. Instead of recognizing that He gives His grace freely to you, you will be constantly attempting to prove to God that you merit His favor.

Larry Crabb insightfully encapsulates our plight in *Inside Out*:

> Fallen man has taken command of his own life, determined above all else to prove that he's adequate for the job. And like the teen who feels rich until he starts paying for his own car insurance, we remain confident of our ability to manage life until we face the reality of our own soul. Nothing is more humbling than the recognition of (1) a deep thirst that makes us entirely dependent on someone else for satisfaction and (2) a depth of corruption that stains everything we do—even

our efforts to reform—with selfishness. To realistically face what is true within us puts us in touch with a level of helplessness we don't care to experience.[2]

Mephibosheth must have known that feeling of helplessness. After all, what could he possibly do for the king? He was crippled in both feet. When David imposed his loving grace upon Mephibosheth, all he could do was admit his absolute helplessness and accept the king's unmerited but boundless love and grace.

Don't you hate that? I do. Accepting God's grace comes hard for me, not that I'd want to stand in His presence for a milli-second on my own merit. It's just that, well, I feel so helpless in His presence and I'm a performance-oriented sort of guy. Although I know better and have even written books advising others in this area, if I am not extremely careful, I find that I begin to base my self-image on what I do or what I have accomplished.

If I can't look back over the day and see some measurable progress, I feel I have wasted a day of my life. That's why I often prefer to mow the lawn or wax the car than write a book. Although the household tasks are tedious, at least the results are immediately visible and measurable.

I must constantly remind myself that it is not what I do for Jesus that gets me into heaven; it is what He has already done on the cross.

Yes, I do things for Him out of a heart of love, an attitude of gratitude and a desire to please Him. But I no longer do these things as I once did—to gain His approval. As a Christian, I live my life *from* His approval, not *for* His approval. What a difference!

Failure to learn this lesson will perpetually frustrate your walk with God. So much so that you may even be tempted to give up and quit . . . like Artie . . .

11

Spiritual Indifference

He wanted nothing to do with God, the church or anything Christian. His heart had grown cold...

Artie stirred his coffee for the third time in less than a minute. He wasn't drinking it; he was simply staring into the brown liquid, his hand idly tapping the spoon against the saucer. His shoulders were slumped and his left elbow leaned heavily on the coffee-shop table in a right angle so Artie could prop up his head.

"I just don't care anymore, Ken," he spoke quietly but bitterly. "I'm numb. I don't feel a thing." Artie rubbed the back of his hand against his eye, wiping away the tears that betrayed his words.

"I don't understand it," he continued. "Jenny prayed for me to become a Christian for all those years. And I was not easy to live with. Drinking and carousing, coming in all hours of the night. But I always knew Jenny loved me, and she was praying for me.

"Two years ago, I gave my life to Christ and what a difference He made. I started going to church as often as I could—three, sometimes four services a week. Even though

I was working sixty hours a week, I got up every Sunday morning and we went to Sunday school with our four kids. It works. I mean, for the first time in our marriage, we were a family.

"Then, all of a sudden, Jenny decides she doesn't want to be married anymore. Not only does she not want to be a wife and a mother, she says she's through with Christianity, too. I tried to get her to go see the pastor with me, but she wouldn't. She left. Just took off one afternoon while I was at work and the kids were in school. She wrote a note—said she had to go find herself. Find herself? I mean, the woman is thirty-seven years old! Shouldn't she have found herself before now?"

Artie stirred his coffee too fast and it swirled out of the cup, spilling onto the table and into his lap. He swished it off his jeans as though it hardly bothered him.

"Anyway, I quit. I've given up praying that she'll come back. I gave it my best shot, and what did I get besides abuse?

"I poured myself into the work of the Lord—or at least I *thought* it was the Lord's work—and I don't have anything to show for it but a tired body, an empty wallet and a bruised spirit. I try being a good Christian husband and father, and I end up raisin' four kids by myself.

"I don't mind telling you, I've been knocked down flat. Frankly, I don't care if I ever get up again. Just let me alone, Ken. Let me bury myself in my work, or in my house, or in front of the TV. Maybe I'll just stay in bed. I don't feel as though I have a reason to get up."

My friend was in a dangerous state. He had passed through the anger stage, screaming obscenities at the door his wife had gone through and not come back. He had dallied in denial for a period of time, refusing to accept that Jenny had left him with four children to care for.

And now Artie's disappointment, despair and disillusionment had brought him to an even more precarious precipice. Suffering from severe depression, for which I encouraged him to seek professional help, Artie honestly felt that he didn't care anymore about Jenny, his children or himself. He wanted nothing to do with God, the church or anything Christian. His heart had grown cold; he was spiritually indifferent.

Most psychologists agree that the opposite of love is not hate; it's indifference. For example, a couple having marital problems has a better chance of reconciliation if there are feelings between them, regardless how negative or bitter those feelings are. But if the couple is indifferent in their feelings, it will take serious, long-term work to recapture the love they once knew. Sadly, many marriages die the agonizing, slow death brought on by indifference.

The same is true spiritually. Indifference is a killer. Even negative reactions are better than no reaction. If you sense yourself sliding toward spiritual indifference, you must take radical corrective action . . . *immediately.*

An Ounce of Prevention

In writing to a group of depressed, disappointed, stressed out, ready-to-quit believers, the apostle Paul emphatically declared, "We do not lose heart!" (2 Corinthians 4:1) Paul's implication is clear: "Don't you lose heart either. If we can make it, so can you!" To help bolster the faith of the beleaguered believers to whom he is writing, the apostle shares a bit of his personal testimony:

> We are afflicted in every way, but not crushed; perplexed, but not despairing; persecuted, but not forsaken; struck down, but not destroyed; always carrying about in the body the dying of Jesus, that the life of Jesus also may be manifested in our body (2 Corinthians 4:8-10).

Despite the fact that Paul was "pressed on every side," not a line of self-pity protrudes from this passage. In fact, unlike many modern preachers and teachers, the apostle Paul never gave the impression that the Christian life was a means of eliminating pressure, worry or pain. Neither did he foist false hope upon half-hearted, fickle followers of Jesus. Paul was a realist. He was saying, "Look, I've been knocked down, but I've never been knocked *out*. And you need not be either."

Nowadays, it is easy to get the impression that all you have to do is become a Christian and you will bounce merrily along from one mountaintop experience to the next. The problem with that sort of teaching is that it simply isn't true; it's a *lie*! The Christian life is not a playground; it is a battlefield with eternal consequences at stake.

Yes, Jesus has already won the war by dying on the cross and rising victoriously from the grave three days later, but the enemy refuses to admit defeat. Satan, although vanquished, will not roll over and play dead. He continues to fight for your soul and will do so until his final punishment is inflicted (Revelation 20:10).

Satanic opposition notwithstanding, let's face it: Life is tough and it takes its toll. We live in an evil, imperfect world where it is not always easy to live for Jesus. Enjoyable? Oh, yes. Meaningful, fulfilling and satisfying? Yes, that too. But simple, never.

One of my favorite books is Hannah Whitall Smith's *The Christian's Secret of a Happy Life*. Written in 1874 by a forty-three-year-old housewife, the book has benefited millions of readers. It is a practical guide to dealing with the unhappiness and uncertainties of life in a spiritually strong, confident, serene manner. The book is a classic, known and loved around the world.

Lesser known is the fact that Hannah's book was published the same year that her husband, Robert, was forced to leave the ministry over his alleged extramarital affairs. Robert had often lashed out at Hannah for her lack of sexual responsiveness. He said, "I need love from a wife. I need warmth and touching and tenderness. Thee is like a dry old stick!"

A young woman approached Robert Smith at a spiritual conference in which he was participating. The story goes:

> In a state of spiritual anguish, she said she needed a counselor to talk to. She invited Robert to her room. "I thought at the time that was not quite proper," Robert confessed later, "but her spiritual distress seemed so great."
>
> He tried to soothe the sobbing woman by sitting down beside her on the bed, putting his arm around her, and talking of spiritual things. According to Robert, that was all that happened. According to the woman, Robert had tried to make love to her . . . .
>
> The head of the conference took immediate action. Robert was summoned into his office the next morning and was told that all his meetings in England were being cancelled. . . . The local newspaper ran this headline: "Famous Evangelist Found in Bedroom of Adoring Female Follower."[1]

Robert was eventually vindicated of improprieties in this case, but Hannah's trust in him had been severely eroded. Her misgivings later proved true as Robert became more flagrant about his immorality. The couple remained married, however, until Robert died in 1898 at the age of seventy-two. Maybe that is why, in her seventies, Hannah wrote, "It is hard for me to believe that any husband and wife are really happy together." This from the woman whose fame rested upon *The Christian's Secret of a Happy Life*!

Hannah did not have a happy life by modern Christian

standards. In addition to her frustration over her marriage, Hannah's youngest daughter married the brilliant but atheistic philosopher Bertrand Russell. According to biographer Marie Henry, Hannah's daughter's faith did not last more than a month after their marriage. They divorced eight years later.

Hannah's oldest daughter shocked society by leaving her husband and traipsing across Europe in an immoral affair with her art teacher. Four of Hannah's children died. Her middle surviving son gave up his faith at age eleven.

In the midst of all this, Hannah wrote in her book *Every Day Religion*:

> Trouble and sorrow, therefore, are not our curse, but one of our most cherished rights. We are like statues, which can only be shaped by the chisel's blows. . . . Why should we allow ourselves to be so needlessly unhappy with thinking that our trouble is one in which God has no part?[2]

What a far cry from modern misconceptions concerning the Christian life. Hannah Whitall Smith could be *happy* (in the best sense of the word) because she did not depend upon external events, people or things to make her happy. Her happiness was the natural by-product of her personal relationship with Christ.

Furthermore, she had what many present-day believers have lost: She had a future-orientation about her faith. This was not some pie-in-the-sky theology, but a calm assurance that life on this earth was only a preview of the main event in eternity. Nowadays, we want instant gratification and we want it yesterday! In *Inside Out*, Larry Crabb insightfully notes:

> We want something *now*! And something is available now, something wonderful and real. But we will only find its counterfeit until we realize that the intensity of our disappointment with life coupled with a Christianity

that promises to relieve that disappointment now has radically shifted the foundation of our faith. No longer do we resolutely bank everything on the coming of a nail-scarred Christ for His groaning but faithfully waiting people. Our hope has switched to a responsive Christ who satisfies His hurting people by quickly granting them the relief they demand.

That hope, however, is a lie, an appealing but grotesque perversion of the good news of Christ. It's a lie responsible for leading hundreds of thousands of seeking people into either a powerless lifestyle of denial and fabricated joy or a turning away from Christianity in disillusionment and disgust.[3]

Clearly, the Bible describes a victorious Christian life, but that life is not exempt from troubles, tragedies or tough problems as some would have you believe. Besides, when you think of it, the only way you can have a victorious Christian life is by having some obstacles to overcome.

Let's Get Real

The apostle Paul understands what it is like to feel down and out. He would say, "I know what it's like to be pressed. At times, I felt as though the entire New York Giants defense was blitzing! No matter where I looked, it was an Excedrin headache coming my way. People were grabbing, pulling, pressuring. It seemed the whole world was out to get me. Sure, they've knocked me down a few times, but they haven't been able to keep me down!"

Paul's encouragement rings true because he knows what he's talking about. He is not simply spouting spiritual tripe. His message is, "Keep on! This Christian life is rocky and rough, but it is real. And you *can* survive; you can thrive. With Christ as your source, you can make it through those dark, lonely hours. You can make it not only to heaven, but you can make it till next Tuesday!"

In the early years of his Christian life, Paul was

witnessing about Jesus in Damascus, and the Jews who were living in these regions became angry because Paul kept proving to them that Jesus was the Messiah (Acts 9:20-25). Their envy soon turned virulent which led to violence. They plotted to kill Paul. Fortunately, Paul learned of the plans in time to make a hasty escape in a basket let down over the city walls. Paul knew what it was like to be surrounded by enemies on every side.

Toward the end of Paul's life, his preaching in Jerusalem stirred up so much trouble that the Roman commander tossed him in prison, primarily to prevent Paul from being torn apart by the rioting crowd who disagreed with his message. Again, a plot was hatched to destroy the apostle. To avoid further conflict, the prison authorities called out two hundred members of the infantry along with seventy horsemen and two hundred others with spears, bows and arrows—all to provide a police escort to Caesarea for the puny preacher (Acts 23:12*ff*). "Pressed," Paul would say, "but not crushed."

Paul also described himself as being "perplexed, but not despairing." The Greek word Paul used for "perplexed" means "strained; stretched until almost ready to snap." Have you ever felt that way? Of course. Every parent knows what it means to have his or her patience stretched to the breaking point. Perhaps you are financially stretched, constantly trying to earn more money to provide for your family. Many are emotionally stretched these days.

During one of the many scandals that plagued the Ronald Reagan presidency, one of his former top cabinet members, Robert McFarlane, attempted to commit suicide by overdosing on Valium. After his recovery, reporter Barbara Walters asked him why he had done it. On national television, McFarlane answered, "I thought the world would be a better place without me."

Have you ever known that feeling? That you just

couldn't make it through another day? Paul would say, "I know that feeling!" He writes:

> For we do not want you to be unaware, brethren, of our affliction which came to us in Asia, that we were burdened excessively, beyond our strength, so that we despaired even of life; indeed, we had the sentence of death within ourselves in order that we should not trust in ourselves, but in God who raises the dead; who delivered us from so great a peril of death, and will deliver us, He on whom we have set our hope (2 Corinthians 1:8-10).

Paul's words pulsate with a confidence not in his own strength to deliver himself, but in God's supernatural power.

He also says that he has been "persecuted, but not forsaken; struck down, but not destroyed" (2 Corinthians 4:9). The word Paul chose for "persecuted" means "to be hunted, pursued, hounded." Indeed, from the day Paul had his Damascus road experience, he endured persecution. People hounded him everywhere he went—the Jews, his former friends; the Romans, his former admirers; and frequently other Christians! But Paul never felt that the Lord had forsaken him or given up on him.

Keep On Keeping On

Paul continues his testimony with a description of his ministry:

> Giving no cause for offense in anything, in order that the ministry be not discredited, but in everything commending ourselves as servants of God, in much endurance, in afflictions, in hardships, in distresses, in beatings, in imprisonments, in tumults, in labors, in sleeplessness, in hunger (2 Corinthians 6:3-5).

Is Paul complaining? Was he a charter member of "Whiners for Christ"? No way! He says that as a servant of God, he counted on bitter times coming, but he refused to respond bitterly. Rather, he responded "in purity, in knowledge, in patience, in kindness, in the Holy Spirit, in genuine love, in the word of truth, in the power of God" (2 Corinthians 6:6,7).

You know—precisely the way *you* respond when people persecute and pressure you, right? Uh-huh.

Paul is describing nitty-gritty Christian living. He's talking about *troubles*: physical, mental, emotional and spiritual hassles. He's talking about *hardships* (*afflictions*): real-life problems that seem to defy solutions. He's talking about *distresses*: those situations where you feel as though you are locked in with no way out. Locked into a career that refuses to happen. Locked into unemployment or disability or some other circumstance over which you have little or no control.

Then, just to make certain that the Corinthians do not miss the point, Paul completes his testimony with these words:

> [I've been] beaten times without number, often in danger of death. Five times I received from the Jews thirty-nine lashes. Three times I was beaten with rods, once I was stoned, three times I was shipwrecked, a night and a day I have spent in the deep. I have been on frequent journeys, in dangers from rivers, dangers from robbers, dangers from my countrymen, dangers from the Gentiles, dangers in the city, dangers in the wilderness, dangers on the sea, dangers among false brethren; I have been in labor and hardship, through many sleepless nights, in hunger and thirst, often without food, in cold and exposure. Apart from such external things, there is the daily pressure upon me of concern for all the churches (2 Corinthians 11:23-28).

He is saying, "I've had pressures from my so-called Christian friends. I've been abused by my enemies. On top of that, I've got daily pressures of my work!" Paul would have gone off the scale on a stress test.

How easy it would have been for the apostle to get discouraged or disgusted with other Christians, with God, maybe even with himself. Why didn't he lash out at God? "God! Where are you? What's going on here? This is not the trip I signed up for!"

Paul had every excuse to say, "I've had it! I quit. I don't need this abuse. I was doing perfectly well as a Pharisee. I'm outta here. I'm through!"

But he didn't. Quite the contrary, he says, "Oh, no! We don't lose heart. We keep on enduring. I'm going to persevere. I'm going to keep on keeping on!" Sometimes, that is the last word that disillusioned Christians want to hear. But it is the only word that makes any sense.

Often, when I am counseling with a disillusioned Christian, he or she will say, "Well, yes. But that was the apostle Paul. You expect that sort of attitude from him."

I'll ask, "And why should you be any different?"

"Well, his circumstances are totally different than mine. I mean, if Paul had to walk in *my* shoes, then he'd know what rough is all about!"

- "If Paul had to live with *my* spouse . . . ."
- "If Paul had to put up with *my* parents . . . ."
- "If Paul had to work where I work . . . ."
- "If Paul had to live in this town, then he'd know what *tough* is all about!"

Paul may not have known your particular circumstances, but he does understand what it's like to be pushed to the limit. And his advice to you is the same, no matter what you're going through:

1. Do not lose heart (2 Corinthians 4:1).

2. Endure, no matter what (2 Corinthians 6:4).

Author Stuart Briscoe tells a story about Olin Hendricks, the great preacher, who wanted to take his wife on a safari to the wilds of Africa. Hendricks' wife's idea of roughing it, however, was staying at a hotel without an indoor pool!

Nevertheless, he succeeded in talking her into going with him to Africa. From the moment they arrived on "the dark continent," Mrs. Hendricks hated it. She abhorred Africa and couldn't wait to get out of the country.

One thing about Africa that Olin believed would excite his wife was Victoria Falls. Beautiful, majestic Victoria Falls had a magnificent bronze statue of missionary explorer David Livingstone—the first white man ever to set foot in that part of Africa—overlooking the cataracts. Throughout their trip, Hendricks kept his wife motivated by reminding her that any day now, they were going to see Victoria Falls. Finally, the day came.

Olin took his wife along the falls and out to the edge of the cliff. There was the stately statue of David Livingstone, his arm raised high, his hand shading his eyes as he peered out over the falls.

This was the moment the Hendricks had been waiting for. Ecstatically, Olin turned to his wife and shouted above the din of falling water, "There! There is the great David Livingstone! Look at him peering over the falls. What do you suppose he is thinking?"

Mrs. Hendricks looked at the statue of Livingstone, then back at her husband and shouted, "I think he is thinking, 'I've had it up to *here* with Africa!'"

Maybe that has become one of your favorite sayings these days:

"I've had it up to here with this marriage!"

"I've had it up to here with these kids . . . this job . . . this church . . . Christianity. *Christians!*"

Try this. When you get that "I've had it up to here" feeling, turn it around and say, "Wait a minute! I am being pressed, but with the Lord's help, I will not be crushed.

"I'm stretched, but I'm not going to snap.

"I'm perplexed, but I am not going to despair.

"I'm being persecuted and hounded, but I know that Jesus has not forsaken me.

"I'm knocked down, but I have not been destroyed.

"Sure, I know the pressure is on from the circumstances, and I know there are people who would oppose me at every turn. I've got plenty of stress, but I am not going to worry. In the midst of it all, with Jesus' help, I refuse to lose heart, and *I will endure!*"

That is true Christianity; not the syrupy, smarmy, sickening counterfeit that has been popular of late. Furthermore, Paul says, keep your eye on eternity:

> For momentary, light affliction is producing for us an eternal weight of glory far beyond all comparison, while we look not at the things which are seen, but at the things which are not seen; for the things which are seen are temporal, but the things which are not seen are eternal (2 Corinthians 4:17,18).

Is that really possible? you may be thinking. Of course, it is! It's all a matter of persistence.

Just Do It!

In his book, *Say Yes To Your Potential*, Skip Ross has a chapter titled, "Do It Until."

Until what? I wondered. Until you get there, I discovered as I read.

How long do you keep getting back on your feet when you fall down? Until you stand.

How long do you continue to press toward the goal? Until you've *reached* it or God changes your direction.

Don't kick, gripe and complain. Just do it!

I attended a spectacular ice show not long ago. As the graceful and acrobatic skaters whisked across the ice and twirled through the air, they made their performance appear so easy that I thought, *I bet I could do that!*

Do you have any idea how many times those fabulous skaters must have fallen down before they learned to glide so gracefully across the ice? I think I do . . . now. No doubt, some of those falls were extremely painful. That ice is cold and hard. Some of their spills (like all of mine) were probably terribly embarrassing. But they got back up and got going again, until they made it.

Do it until.

Some people never quite make it in life because they give up too easily. They have all the logical reasons (excuses) why they should quit:

"I don't have enough education."

"My wife and I can't get along."

"I'm too old."

"I'm too young."

"I have a physical disability."

"I don't have enough money."

"I'm from the wrong side of the tracks."

"I'm co-dependent."

"I'm a child of an alcoholic (or a drug addict, or some other compulsion)."

"I was abused as a child."

No doubt many of these excuses are valid. Nevertheless, most of the world's "Horatio Alger" stories belong not to the extremely talented, but to the extremely persistent. Nearly all of them experienced severe failure or misfortune at some point in their lives.

Fanny Crosby, the hymn writer who gave us "Blessed

Assurance (Jesus is mine)," was blind. George Bernard Shaw, the famous writer, had his first five novels rejected. Super-quarterback Joe Montana suffered a shoulder injury that should have sidelined him forever. Richard Wagner, the master music composer, was an abject failure as a musician the first thirty years of his life. His first opera was so awful, he couldn't finish it. His second was so bad nobody would produce it. His third opened and closed the same night. But he kept at it, and history now hails him as one of the world's finest composers.

In the 1950s a father in Wheaton, Illinois, was trying to read the Bible to his children—all ten of them. The kids were bored. They couldn't understand many of the strange-sounding words in the King James Version.

The dad, Ken Taylor, decided he would paraphrase the Bible into language his children could understand. For six years he worked night and day, often while riding a commuter train to and from his job in Chicago. Slowly but surely, he converted parts of the New Testament into a readable paraphrase that even a youngster could understand.

He took his manuscript to a publisher and the publisher turned it down. A second publisher did the same; so did a third. They all said, "Nobody would be interested."

Finally, Ken Taylor took his own savings and published it himself. The first year, he sold a paltry eight hundred copies, not exactly anything to boast about when you consider that the Bible is the all-time bestselling book in the world.

Still, Ken Taylor refused to give up. He knew the Lord had given him an idea and a job to get done. Against all odds, he continued to paraphrase the entire New Testament and eventually completed the entire Bible. He called his paraphrase *The Living Bible,* which today has sold well over twenty-five million copies. It has been a blessing and an evangelistic tool for millions.

Ken Taylor changed the face of history because of his love for his children and because *he would not give up.* He would not lose heart. He kept pressing on.

"But Ken," a sincere man objected after I had spoken at his church about this subject, "how long can a person keep on keeping on? I feel as though I have been in a holding pattern over O'Hare. It's like I called God and He put me on hold, then forgot to come back on the line!"

Ah, the disillusionment caused by *delay.* Now that is a matter we can put off no longer . . .

12

Detours and Delays

Detours and delays never surprise God.
When He allows the interruption of your plans,
it is always on purpose.

Bonnie and Steve are a delightful Christian couple, spiritually mature, financially and emotionally stable. Their marriage is solid and their home centers around Jesus Christ. They lack only one thing, as far as they are able to see. They love children and they have none.

They have sought all sorts of medical assistance, attended fertility classes at a local hospital, and tried every "old wives' tale" that anyone has suggested—all to no avail.

More importantly, they have prayed for the Lord's will to be done regarding their barrenness. Steve says, "I read in the Bible that children are a blessing from the Lord, so we believe we are praying according to God's will. We've prayed over this matter ourselves, and we've been prayed over several times by the elders at our church. Our pastor often invites those couples who are praying to have children to come forward for corporate prayer. We always respond. Still, we are unable to conceive."

Bonnie concurs: "We've thought of adoption and

haven't ruled that option out. Right now, though, we are simply waiting on God and doing our best to have patience. We believe our motives are pure, our hearts are right and we have presented a valid request. The rest is up to Him. We're leaving it in His hands."

Few things are more difficult for a godly man or woman to accept than the discipline of delay. The natural tendency is to look at those things that thwart or interrupt our plans or progress with disdain, disappointment or anger. The why questions race through our minds: "Why this, God? Why now? Why me?"

You have probably discovered by now that God rarely answers the why questions; He is much more interested in the who question: "Who are you going to trust, you or Me?"

Delay is difficult to understand and rarely enjoyable, especially when it seems that the plan you are attempting to implement has a holy, God-honoring purpose. But detours and delays never surprise God. When He allows the interruption of your plans, it is always on purpose.

He may be taking you in a different direction to the place you desire to go. He may be trying to get your attention. The enforced waiting period may be intended to focus your attention on Him rather than your plan. Many times, the delay is allowed so you can align yourself with God's timetable. The phrase, "Timing is everything," is certainly appropriate when you are seeking God's will in your life.

Even when you have a direct promise from the Lord concerning His plan, attempting to manipulate circumstances or events to help fulfill His will may be disastrous.

The Dangers of Doing It My Way

One of my least favorite songs is the classic, "My Way," written by Paul Anka and recorded by everyone from Frank Sinatra to Elvis Presley. It's not the tune that I dislike;

it's the message. God is not interested in you "doing it your way." He demands that you do it *His* way. When you confuse or dilute this important principle, you are going to create some awful messes.

That's precisely what happened to Abraham and his wife Sarah (known as Abram and Sarai until God changed their names). Abraham was perplexed; he had a problem. God had made some specific promises to him, saying:

> I will make you a great nation,
> And I will bless you, and make your name great. . . .
> And in you all the families of the earth shall be blessed
>   (Genesis 12:2,3).

The problem? Abraham and Sarah were childless. How in the world was God going to make his family great when Abraham had no children?

Several years went by and Abraham became impatient. Perhaps he began to doubt God's Word, thinking that he was not going to have a son of his own after all. "When God? Where God? How God? How long am I going to have to wait? God, I'm not getting any younger, you know!" The why questions probably dominated Abraham's thoughts.

He began to consider the possibility of naming his servant Eliezer as his heir, thinking, "Well, maybe God will bless my house through him." But again God spoke specifically to Abraham's situation:

> Then behold, the word of the LORD came to him, saying, "This man will not be your heir; but one who shall come forth from your own body, he shall be your heir." And He took him outside and said, "Now look toward the heavens, and count the stars, if you are able to count them." And He said to him, "So shall your descendants be" (Genesis 15:4,5).

Abraham believed God, but he was still bewildered.

After all, God had promised to give him descendants, but Sarah was still barren. She had never been able to conceive and now she was past the age when women normally get pregnant. Ten more years slipped by and still the promise remained unfulfilled.

Then came the shocker: One day, *Sarah* suggested to Abraham that he have sex with her maid Hagar in order to have children by her (Genesis 16:2). She could become a second wife to Abraham (16:3). While Sarah's suggestion seems atrocious by modern standards, this practice was relatively routine in Mesopotamia at that time. If a wife was barren, she could supply her husband with a slave girl as a concubine. If the slave girl became pregnant, she would deliver the child on the knees of the master's wife, and the child was considered as belonging to the father and his wife.

Still, Sarah's suggestion raises two suspicions. First, Hagar was an Egyptian. She may well have been one of the female stewards that Abraham and Sarah had acquired when they sojourned in Egypt, a trip during which, in order to save his own life, Abraham had pawned off Sarah as his sister and had allowed Pharaoh to take Sarah into his own house. (In case the significance of that "benevolent" gesture slips by you, Pharaoh was not inviting Sarah into his house for a cup of tea. He was bringing her in as one of his concubines!) As a reward, Pharaoh gave Abraham "sheep and oxen and donkeys and male and female servants and female donkeys and camels" (Genesis 12:16). Fortunately, God protected Sarah and allowed her to escape unscathed, but it was a close call.

Obviously, Abraham had not consulted God concerning the wisdom of offering his wife to Pharaoh. Nor did he consult the Lord concerning Sarah's suggestion of having sex with Hagar, the Egyptian servant girl.

Second, Sarah had an unusual willingness to "spiritualize" this entire affair. She says, "The Lord has prevented me from bearing children," which has a slightly accusative tone to it while maintaining a high degree of spirituality. Sarah had not consulted the Lord about the decision concerning Hagar either, but she used that sweet, spiritual-sounding rationale to manipulate other people into doing things her way.

Nowadays, we often hear, "The Lord led me" as an excuse for all sorts of outrageous conduct. I vividly recall a young woman who informed me, "The Lord has led me to marry you!" I thanked her and said as delicately as I could, "That's extremely interesting, but the Lord has *not* led me to marry you." She was quite offended and has questioned my spiritual maturity ever since.

Abraham's Mistakes

Unfortunately, Abraham listened to the subjective, suspect wisdom of Sarah. As a result, he made three major mistakes.

1. *Abraham assumed that Sarah's arguments were valid.* After all, God had not specifically promised that Sarah would be the *mother* of a multitude; only that he, Abraham, would be the *father* of a multitude! Maybe God intended to use this affair with Hagar for good.

Unfortunately, Abraham listened to Sarah's advice without seeking the Lord's direction, and he made a wrong decision.

2. *Abraham assumed that Sarah's suggestion was based on unselfish motives.* As events unfolded, Sarah's attitude proved to be less than noble. Consequently, her solution became another problem rather than a blessing. As Harvey McKay says, "Beware the naked man who offers you his shirt!"

3. Most dangerously, *Abraham allowed the thought patterns and practices of his pagan culture to influence his decision-making process.* Understand, Sarah and

Abraham's actions were totally acceptable and extremely common in those days . . . for ungodly people. But God had plans of doing something wonderfully new in and through this couple. They were people of the promise. Their attitudes and conduct were to be based upon His Word to them, not the latest popular opinion poll. It is always dangerous for God's people to allow sinful society to be the yardstick by which they measure right and wrong. The question for God's people is not, "What does society say?" but rather, "What does *God* say?"

Abraham's impatience produced further complications. When Hagar became pregnant, she also became proud, arrogant and boastful. Scripture says that "when she saw that she had conceived, her mistress was despised in her sight" (Genesis 16:4). That's a nice way of saying Hagar was going around thumbing her nose at Sarah and chiding, "Nya, na, na, na, nyaaa! I got pregnant and you didn't!"

While Hagar's attitude and actions were reprehensible, they were understandable and, perhaps, predictable.

Another result of Abraham's mistake was that Sarah became bitter—and not just toward Hagar, but toward Abraham as well! She lashed out at him, "May the wrong done me be upon you" (16:5). Although she had actually instigated this entire mess, she still blamed Abraham for the indignities done to her.

Abraham's original problem became worse, not better, as a result of his acting presumptuously ahead of the Lord's timing.

Practical Pointers From Abraham's Blunder

In dealing with the delays in your life, take into consideration these five important principles from Abraham's mistake.

1. *Diligently avoid the tendency to take things into your own hands.* You can't blame Abraham for getting

impatient, but the price tag on presumption is always higher than you think it will be.

When you are in a holding pattern, your first question should not be, "What can I do to change this situation?" As admirable as that may sound, the most important question really is: "What does *God* want me to do?" The next step of obedience is all you need to know. Unfortunately, Abraham's impatience caused him to accept a compromise that *seemed* to be the thing to do at the time. He was wrong.

2. *Guard against making quick decisions and snap judgments whenever possible.* Certainly you must think and act quickly and decisively at times. Sometimes, even a wrong decision is better than no decision.

For the most part, though, few major decisions demand that sort of expediency. Don't be in such a hurry. Take as much time as you need to think and pray things through. If you are married, all major decisions need to be discussed between you and your spouse.

After ten years of living in Canaan, Abraham wanted to expedite the program. He may have even felt he was helping God out a bit by having a child with Hagar. Wrong again.

3. *Even those individuals closest to you can lead you astray if you are not careful.* They may not intend to do so. Their motives may be perfectly pure. But sometimes those whom you trust, or those friends and family who love you the most, may offer advice that is not consistent with God's plan for your life. This is often the case when your loved ones see that you are hurt, disheartened or discouraged. In an effort to encourage you, they may inadvertently lead you in the wrong direction.

No doubt, Sarah hurt for Abraham because of her barren womb. In their culture, it was a disgrace for a man not to have a legitimate heir. Nevertheless, her suggestion was a humanistic, man-centered idea that neglected God's plan completely.

4. When you are seeking the will of God, *beware the subtle influences of your former lifestyle and the sin surrounding you.* Abraham and Sarah had come out of a pagan, idol-worshipping background. Perhaps you have a past of which you are not particularly proud. Be careful that your present decisions and opinions are not negatively colored by conduct and concepts of which you have been cleansed and forgiven.

Our culture has a way of creeping into our thinking processes. That's why the maxim, "Let your conscience be your guide," is often a deficient standard. Your conscience has been seared by sin and is not infallible. Better to base your decisions on an absolute standard you can trust: the Word of God.

5. Finally, in charting your course of action, *choose methods and strategies that are in harmony with scriptural guidelines.* When I was a young Christian, I often heard the adage, "The Bible gives the answer for every question." The further along I traveled with the Lord, the more I realized the falsehood of that statement. The Bible does not answer *every* question of life. For example, the Word says absolutely nothing about how to run my computer or which stocks to invest in or how to fix a leaking faucet or how to set the timer on my VCR. I have questions about all of those things.

God will not always give you specific directions for making particular decisions. He gives you guiding principles and real-life illustrations of them. Then He expects you to use your sanctified common sense to make wise decisions.

That's why it is imperative to never select a method of dealing with your delay that contradicts His revealed Word to you. If you do, you will only compound your problems.

When the Enemy Is You!

In a sense, Abraham was his own worst enemy. No doubt, he was sincere in his desire to do God's will, but his perspective was clouded by impatience and helped along by Sarah's suggestion and sinful society's support for his actions.

By all human logic, it was easy for Abraham to conclude that Hagar would be the mother of his son. But his logic was wrong; that was not God's plan.

Hagar did bear a son, Ishmael, but he was not the fulfillment of the promise God had made to Abraham. Moreover, from the moment that Hagar and Abraham's son was conceived, Abraham's life, his wife's life and the lives of everyone around them were thrown into chaos and confusion. The conflict between the sons of Abraham—Arab versus Jew—continues to this day.

After Hagar conceived, Sarah treated her so harshly that Hagar fled to the wilderness. The angel of the Lord found Hagar and comforted her by promising:

> I will greatly multiply your descendants so that they shall be too many to count (Genesis 16:10).

Can you imagine Abraham's confusion when he heard about *that?* After all, God's promise to multiply Hagar's and his offspring through Ishmael *sounded* so much like the Lord's previous promise to Abraham. Maybe this was another confirmation!

Sadly, Abraham's errors continued to multiply. God's message to Hagar—and notice, the message was to Hagar, not to Abraham—led Abraham to leap to another false conclusion. Namely, that he had done the *right* thing in delaying no longer the evidence of his reproductive prowess; his helpful nudge had brought Ishmael into the world through Hagar. It must be God's will.

Notice again the subtle deception:

- Abraham was so sincere.

- His decision seemed so logical.

- A son was actually born.

- God's promise to Hagar sounded so similar to God's promise to him.

Abraham *assumed* he was walking in the center of God's will for his life. But by taking things into his own hands, Abraham was soon to learn one of the most difficult lessons a child of God can learn. God let him wander in the wilderness of his own mistakes *for the next thirteen years!* Abraham was eighty-six years old at the conception of Ishmael, and the Bible does not mention that God spoke to him again until he was ninety-nine (Genesis 17:1).

For thirteen years, it seemed to Abraham that the heavens were brass. Worse still, during that entire time, Abraham probably thought he was in the will of God! How painful it must have been for him to discover that he had been so deluded.

God was teaching Abraham an important lesson: When a child of God takes things into his or her own hands and attempts to manipulate people, relationships or situations, *God will allow him to do it.* He may not even say a word. Then He will allow His child to struggle through the darkness and foolishness he or she has created.

Thankfully, God's grace is greater than our foolishness and He is able to clean up the messes we make. If you have learned the lesson God has been trying to teach you through delays and detours, you will probably be more than ready to listen to Him the next time He speaks. That's what happened in Abraham's life, and the next word he received from God was the promise that within a year their long awaited son would be born . . . and God kept His promise.

He will keep His promises to you.

13

In the Dungeon of Delay

Endurance does not mean, "I'll just hang in there until Jesus comes." Endurance means, "I believe that what God said He would do, He will, in fact, do!"

Not everyone handles delay well. We want to learn patience—yesterday! I put a cup of coffee in the microwave oven, set the timer for two minutes and then start pacing! It's the same old story: We want what we want and we want it now!

John, thirty-three years of age, was having difficulty being patient while waiting for God to provide him with a mate. He bounced his affections from one woman to the next, never allowing himself to get too near the marriage ceremony. He was handsome and bright, and he held a master's degree from Oxford. He was a minister and the son of a minister. He was even a missionary.

John was perplexed. While he was intent on pursuing personal holiness on the mission field, he had not anticipated such a beautiful stumbling block as Sophy Hopkey, the eighteen-year-old niece of the local magistrate. Sophy was everything John wanted in a woman. She was physically attractive, mentally alert and deeply interested in spiritual things. During many of their "dates," John read books of sermons to her.

Still, John had a problem. When he was with Sophy, he confessed that he was under the weight of "an unholy desire." Part of John wanted to marry Sophy, but part of him was afraid to make the commitment. He decided to stay away from her for a while to seek God's direction. When no distinct answer came, John decided to do what they did in Bible days. He drew lots. He took three separate slips of paper and wrote "Marry" on one, "Not this year" on another, and "Think of it no more" on the third. John drew the third slip of paper.

Heartbroken and confused, yet with a sense of relief, John broke off his relationship with Sophy, creating quite a stir in town. Everyone, including Sophy's uncle, felt certain the two would marry. It was no small scandal. In fact, John soon left town, his ministry and life a shambles, and sailed for home. He had lasted less than two years as a missionary. Although he and his brother Charles became dominant figures in eighteenth century Christianity, John Wesley carried with him a sense of disillusionment the rest of his life.

At age forty-seven, John married Molly Vazeille after a courtship of only sixteen days. Their marriage was a disaster. Though they stayed married, they separated for long periods of time on several occasions during their marriage. In 1776, when he was seventy-three and she sixty-seven, "they separated for the last time. 'The water is spilt,' John wrote, 'and it cannot be gathered up again.' "[1]

Like the patriarch Abraham, John Wesley's impatience and presumption carried with it a high price tag.

The Incredible Commitment of Joseph

While Abraham is an example of presumption and manipulation in the midst of delay, his great-grandson

Joseph is the model of patiently trusting God despite the darkness, despair and disappointment of a dungeon experience.

You may recall that Joseph was put in a pit by his own brothers. As if that were not bad enough, they then sold him into slavery. And all of this because "Joseph had a dream" (Genesis 37:5). Actually, Joseph had several dreams that indicated the same thing: God would bless his life and place him in a position of leadership and authority.

Although Joseph's wisdom in sharing his vision with his parents and brothers is questionable, his commitment to, and confidence in, that God-given dream was indefatigable. Even when he was betrayed by his brothers, sold into slavery and put into prison after being falsely accused of rape by Potiphar's wife, Joseph never abandoned his dream.

Much has been written about Joseph's godly character. He seemed to do almost everything just right. He refused to yield to temptations which millions of other men have succumbed to: money, sex and power. He maintained a positive attitude in the midst of the dungeons of Egypt, apparently never doubting or giving up under the pressure. He said all the right things and made all the right moves. Even when his dream was fulfilled, he refused to flaunt his success in the faces of his family members who had flagrantly offended him. What a guy!

It is precisely because Joseph does seem so "perfect" that you can find encouragement in the midst of your detours and delays. After all, if God was going to give a rush response to anyone's prayer request, He would surely do so for a fellow such as Joseph. But He didn't. In fact, God had Joseph on hold for more than half of his lifetime.

Delay, however, is never idle downtime with God. It is always preparatory; it has purpose. If you are in a dungeon of delay, do not dismiss it as wasted time. God is preparing you for some divine purpose.

Still, Joseph's commitment is incredible. How he must have been tempted to deny the word of God that had been revealed to him. As Joseph watched the days turn into weeks, then months, then years, Satan must have whispered, "Joseph, if you will only admit that you never really had those dreams! Or at least admit that you may have misinterpreted God's message. Surely, it must have been someone else's voice you heard. It couldn't have been God speaking to you."

Don Stephens headed up Youth With a Mission's project to purchase and renovate a huge, old, eleven thousand ton passenger ship to be used as a hospital ship with an evangelistic outreach. During the long, arduous process, numerous people, many of them strong Christian believers and some even friends, rebuked the YWAM team for biting off more than they could chew. They said, "If you would only admit that you have never really heard from God about having a ministry ship, things would go so much better for you."

But Don Stephens and Loren Cunningham and others at YWAM were certain they had received a vision from God. On July 7, 1982, after months of knuckle-grinding work to get the ship seaworthy, the crew pulled up anchor and set sail from Greece. The ship's name, The *Anastasis*, means resurrection.

Time Is On God's Side

It was thirty years before God's vision to Joseph came to fruition, but when it did, the timing was perfect. Because of his God-given ability to interpret Pharaoh's dreams, Joseph was exalted to the second highest position in the land of Egypt. God had been preparing him all those years to be an instrument of mercy to his family and also, in a sense, God placed Joseph in the perfect position to bring salvation to his family, to their nation, to Egypt and to the world.

God often uses delay to build character into His people. He also uses delay as a time of preparation. And delay is always designed to fulfill His purposes.

One day Lazarus, a good friend of Jesus', took sick. His sisters, Mary and Martha, immediately sent word to Jesus, hoping that He would come to their home quickly. In writing about this event, John notes:

> Now Jesus loved Martha, and her sister, and Lazarus. When therefore He heard that he was sick, He stayed then two days longer in the place where He was (John 11:5,6).

Wait a minute! If Jesus loved Lazarus and his sisters so much, why would He delay two whole days before going to them? The disciples had their own set of questions, but Jesus stated His position clearly: "Lazarus is dead, and I am glad for your sakes that I was not there, so that you may believe; but let us go to him" (John 11:14,15).

By the time Jesus and the disciples arrived at the home of His friends in Bethany, Lazarus had already been dead four days. Martha came out to meet the master and said, "Lord, if You had been here, my brother would not have died. Even now I know that whatever You ask of God, God will give You" (John 11:21).

Undoubtedly, Martha veiled an accusation in her comment: "Jesus, where *were* You? If only you would have come when I called You, none of this would have happened! Why didn't You do it my way?"

Mary said the same thing, "Lord, if You had been here, my brother would not have died" (John 11:32).

But God does His work, His way, for His purposes, in His own time.

Jesus said to Martha, "Your brother shall rise again"

(John 11:23). He went to the tomb, past the professional mourners and the Jewish critics, and ordered the stone to be removed.

Martha objected: "Lord, by this time there will be a stench. He has been dead four days."

Jesus said to her, "Did I not say to you, if you believe, you will see the glory of God?" (John 11:39,40)

The Lord's promise to Mary and Martha is valid for you. If you believe what He has spoken to you, there will come a day when delays will be done, when you are propelled out of that dark prison and into the position in which God wants to use you for His glory.

If you believe Him.

Jesus said, "Lazarus, come forth!" and Lazarus did!

> He who had died came forth, bound hand and foot with wrappings; and his face was wrapped around with a cloth. Jesus said to them, "Unbind him, and let him go" (John 11:44).

If God has placed a dream in your heart, do not give up. Be diligent. Endure even in the dungeons of life.

Our generation knows little about endurance; we are so accustomed to instant gratification. Endurance does not mean, "I'll just hang in there until Jesus comes." Endurance means, "I believe that what God said He would do, He will, in fact, do!" Endurance means that you can say with the ancient prophet Habakkuk,

> Though the fig tree should not blossom, and there be no fruit on the vines, though the yield of the olive should fail, and the fields produce no food, though the flocks should be cut off from the fold, and there be no cattle in the stalls, yet I will exalt in the LORD, I will rejoice in the God of my salvation. The LORD GOD is my strength, and He has made my feet like hinds' feet, and makes me walk on my high places (Habakkuk 3:17-19).

That is what endurance is all about!

Your days of preparation may even now be nearing an end. The delay you have endured has not been an accident, but was according to His plan and for His purposes. Soon the Lord will be standing outside your dream or the vision He has given you, and you will hear, "Come forth!"

Perhaps you have been a friend of Jesus' for a long time, but recently you feel you have been spiritually dead, a form wrapped in the grave clothes of doubt, discouragement, depression and disillusionment. Today, hear His voice as He speaks to you, "My child, come forth!"

14

Falling Off
the Mountaintop

*"Sometimes I feel like just jumping in the car,
taking off and never coming back."*

I placed my breakfast tray on the kitchen counter of the rustic retreat center where I was the speaker for a spiritual renewal weekend. As I turned around, I bumped right into a rugged, bearded fellow. Dressed in a flannel shirt, blue jeans and hiking boots, he looked as much at home in this mountain setting as Daniel Boone. His name tag identified him as "Tim," but I immediately recognized him as the big guy who had sat slouched in his chair all through last night's sessions. He had not spoken a word all evening and looked as though he was bored with the whole affair.

"Oh, man, I'm sorry, Tim," I blurted out. "I didn't even see you there."

"No problem," he answered gruffly, and then his voice softened to a whisper. "Got a minute? I need to talk to you."

I glanced quickly at my watch, knowing that I had only a few minutes before the morning session was to begin. But something in Tim's eyes and the urgency in his voice caused me to say, "Yeah, sure, I've got a few minutes. Let's sit down over here by the fireplace." I believe now the Holy Spirit prompted me to realize the seriousness of Tim's condition.

We sat down on two chairs facing each other in front of the fireplace.

"I feel like I'm ready to crack," he began. "I can't give you one specific reason. It just seems to be an assortment of things piling on me. I've got a beautiful wife and three kids that any guy would be proud of, a nice house and a good job. And I'm about ready to throw it all away."

"Is there another woman?" I asked Tim straightforwardly, assuming he was running around on his wife.

My directness surprised him, but I could tell he appreciated my no-nonsense approach. He relaxed, leaned back, crossed one leg over the other and almost smiled as he answered, "No, no. Nothing like that. I've had women come on to me at work, but I've got a Rolls Royce at home. Why would I want to waste my time with a Yugo?"

I nodded in understanding. I was beginning to like this guy.

"It's just that everything has been getting to me lately," Tim went on. "For no apparent reason, I'm discouraged and depressed most of the time. Then I get disgusted for being so down. Whenever anybody asks me how I'm doing, I always say 'Fine.' But sometimes, I feel like just jumping in the car, taking off and never coming back."

As Tim talked, my heart went out to him and I lost track of the time. The retreat leaders kindly started the morning session without me as Tim told his story.

He was a genuinely nice guy, a good family man, a faithful member of his church and a hard worker on the job. Yet due to the depressed economy in his part of the country, he was about to be laid off from work. He loved his wife and kids, and worked long, hard hours to provide for them.

For a variety of reasons, however, he and his wife were having marital problems. He received little love and affection from his wife and he expressed none to her. They slept in separate rooms.

With tears in his eyes, Tim told me that if something didn't happen to turn things around this weekend, he was going to file for divorce. It was already Saturday morning.

"I just don't understand," he whispered. "I've done the best I can, better than a lot of guys I know. But my life isn't working. What's wrong with me, Ken? If God really cares, how could He allow this to happen?"

As I was about to open my mouth to answer, a loud, crackling, popping sound came from the fireplace. Tim and I glanced in the direction of the hearth. The fire that had been burning so robustly when we first sat down had now burned to a few embers that glowed intermittently as though gasping for breath. All that remained of the fire was a smoldering pile of ashes.

"Do you see those ashes?" Tim asked as he pointed in their direction. I nodded. "That's what my life feels like right now. The fire has just about gone out."

Tim and I talked for another half hour. I gave him some passages of Scripture to read that I thought might encourage him. Then we prayed together and walked on down to the meeting room where the others were having their mid-morning coffee break. Because everyone was milling about and talking, we entered the room almost unnoticed. Tim walked directly across the room, sat down next to his wife Joan and began talking quietly with her.

Later that morning, at the conclusion of my session with the group, I asked if there was anyone who wanted us to pray for them. Tim spoke aloud, "I do," and Joan echoed him, "I do, too." Together the couple pulled their chairs into the center of the room, and the group gathered around them to pray.

Before anyone else could begin, Tim broke down and began to cry. He spoke cautiously but straightforwardly about the condition of his heart. He discreetly revealed just enough details to let everyone know that his marriage was in trouble. Joan nodded her head in agreement as the couple tightly held hands in the middle of our circle. Both Tim and Joan spoke candidly about their concerns for their financial, emotional and spiritual future.

Nobody in the circle laughed. Nobody said, "How could you feel that way?" Several individuals began sobbing; others were crying outright. People placed their hands on Tim and Joan's shoulders and began praying for them. Others knelt on the floor and prayed. It was not a noisy, fanatical type of prayer meeting—just a sweet, fresh wave of God's Spirit moving across the room.

When we finished praying for Tim and Joan, someone else asked, "Would you pray for me?" and the fires of true revival continued.

God did a marvelous miracle in Tim and Joan's lives that day. It wasn't the cure-all for their problems, but He healed many of the hurts they had been experiencing in their marriage and He worked in them individually as well. He reignited a fire that had nearly been extinguished through neglect. He rekindled a flame for each other and for Him within both their hearts.

When we finally returned to the dining room for lunch, the first thing we noticed was that someone had stoked the dying embers in the fireplace and added some fresh wood. The fire was blazing again.

You're in Good Company

Maybe you can identify with Tim and Joan. Perhaps you're burned out, discouraged or disillusioned even as you read these pages. Or possibly you have experienced those feelings in the past, and to be perfectly honest, you have no idea how you ever survived. And you're not quite sure what to do if or when those attacks come again.

Beyond that, you may have friends or family members who have been decimated in recent months due to depression, discouragement or disillusionment. You want to help them, but you're not exactly sure where to start.

You may be surprised to know that many of the great saints suffered from this sort of depression. If you explore recent church history, you will discover many of the believers whose sermons, hymns and books we now regard as classics were frequently depressed.

The "prince of preachers," Charles Haddon Spurgeon, was often so down and discouraged that somebody had to coax him to get into the pulpit to preach. He penned poignantly, "The strong are not always ready, the brave not always courageous, and the joyous not always happy."[1] Though he preached to thousands, Spurgeon often thought of quitting the ministry.

I once asked a prominent pastor, "Have you ever thought about getting out of the ministry?"

Without hesitation, he responded, "Yep. About three times every week!"

And the faithful followers in the Bible were not exempt. Moses, for instance, became so frustrated with the job God had called him to do, and the people with whom he had to work, that he asked God to kill him!

> So Moses said to the LORD, "Why hast Thou been so hard on Thy servant? And why have I not found favor in Thy sight, that Thou hast laid the burden of all this people on me? . . . So if Thou art going to deal thus with me, please kill me at once, if I have found favor in Thy sight, and do not let me see my wretchedness" (Numbers 11:11,15).

Whew! Talk about depression and discouragement!

Do you remember the Old Testament character Job? He received the ultimate compliment from the Lord:

> The Lord said to Satan, "Have you considered My servant Job? For there is no one like him on the earth, a blameless and upright man, fearing God and turning away from evil" (Job 1:8).

But a short time later, when his world was crumbling and his body was being smitten by Satanic attack, Job cursed the day he was born (Job 3:1-3).

David loved the Lord and was described as a man after God's own heart. He wrote psalms that have inspired men and women for generations. But David also wrote many psalms as despairing cries for help, honestly reflecting his attitude during times of deep discouragement. His language in these psalms is not soft and pastoral, but bold, brash and blunt. Many times as I am reading one of David's psalms, I almost want to say, "Whoa, David! Don't talk like that! God's gonna get you." Yet God never zapped David for expressing his true feelings. Nor did He send down fire and brimstone upon Moses or Job for their outbursts (though He did thoroughly rebuke all three of His men at one time or another).

I've discovered that the Lord rarely reprimands me for expressing my disappointments, doubts or fears. At times I have said, "God, I just don't understand. This makes no sense to me. Why has this happened (or not happened)? What in the world am I doing here?" I've learned some hard lessons whenever I've allowed my questions and doubts to turn into disbelief, though, or when I have foolishly permitted my expressions of discontent to turn into irreverence or disrespect for His holiness.

Certainly when you are down and out, God is not going to heap further condemnation upon you for honestly expressing the things you are feeling in your heart and mind. Nevertheless, be careful that in your low times you don't

say things to God, friends, family or your spouse that you
will later regret.

An Imperfect Hero

If you are prone to depression and burnout, please
understand: You are not alone. It is not necessarily a sin to
become depressed; it happens to even the most devout men
and women, people in whom and through whom God has
performed miraculous wonders. The prophet Elijah was
such a person.

Elijah is well known for his great faith in God and his
miraculous feats done in the name of the Lord. But he could
be just as well known for his fears, awful frustrations and
deep despair.

Elijah's name means, "the Lord is God." The first time
we see him in the Bible, he is in the office of wicked King
Ahab boldly proclaiming, "You may run this country, buddy,
but it isn't going to rain again until I say so!" And it didn't.
The rains ceased, and the hot Middle-Eastern sun beat down
incessantly. Soon the crops wilted in the fields, water
supplies ran dangerously low and the lush lands of Israel
turned into barren deadness.

God divinely provided for Elijah during this time by
sending ravens to feed him alongside a brook. After a while,
though, the brook dried up and the ravens quit coming.
Then the Lord sent Elijah to a widow in Zarephath, where
once again God supernaturally provided for him. Elijah
witnessed several specific object lessons to remind him of
the Lord's loving ability to take care of him.

That may explain his boldness in instigating a show-
down on Mount Carmel. He faced the 450 prophets of Baal
and the 400 prophets of the Asherah who were operating
under the direct auspices of sleazy Queen Jezebel, the wife
of the King of Israel.

On Mount Carmel, Elijah presented his peak performance. Little children still tell the story of how he challenged the prophets of Baal to call down fire from heaven to consume a prepared sacrifice. And what Sunday school student could ever forget Elijah's powerful exhortation to the people of Israel: "How long will you hesitate between two opinions? If the Lord is God, follow Him; but if Baal, follow him" (1 Kings 18:21).

When the false gods failed to consume the sacrifice, Elijah prayed a simple prayer to the one true God, and the fire fell! "And when all the people saw it, they fell on their faces; and they said, 'The LORD, He is God; the LORD, He is God' " (18:39).

Elijah, having proven his point, commanded the people to seize the false prophets and slaughter them. Then he almost arrogantly instructed Ahab to get out his umbrella because it was going to pour! Talk about confidence in God! Elijah told this to Ahab *before* he had even prayed about it. Then after the man of God prayed, he sent his servant back to Ahab with the message: "Prepare your chariot and go down, so that the heavy shower does not stop you" (1 Kings 18:44). He was saying to Ahab, "You better get going Ahab. I don't want you to get stuck in the mud!"

Mud? What mud? It hadn't rained for three-and-a-half years. The entire area was a dustbowl! But no sooner had Elijah said it than the dark rain clouds rolled in and the heavy showers began to fall.

Ahab jumped into his chariot and hightailed it back to Jezreel. Meanwhile Elijah, traveling on foot, outran him! Was he on steroids or what? Well, according to Scripture, "The hand of the Lord was on Elijah" (1 Kings 18:46). At this point, Elijah was on a roll. His adrenalin level must have been bouncing off the ceiling. What an incredible spiritual high!

But then Ahab told Jezebel all that Elijah had done: how he had first embarrassed and then killed the prophets of Baal. When Jezebel heard this report, she flew into a fury. She sent a message to Elijah saying, "So may the gods do to me and even more, if I do not make your life as the life of one of them by tomorrow about this time" (1 Kings 19:2).

When Elijah heard the words of this woman, "he was afraid and arose and ran for his life" (1 Kings 19:3).

No doubt, Jezebel's threats dashed Elijah's great expectations. After all, he had successfully challenged and defeated the prophets of Baal in the name of the Lord. In only a few days he had gone from obscurity to national recognition. The people of Israel had rallied around him in destroying the false prophets. If anybody, Jezebel should be the one running for her life!

Elijah may have thought, *God? This wasn't the way the professors in prophet-school taught us that things would work! After all I have done for You, Lord, it's not supposed to happen like this. I mean, I thought Jezebel and Ahab would publicly repent and we'd have a mighty national revival. Maybe we could even elect some godly public officials, get the filth and perversion off our streets, get the Bible back in our schools . . . Lord?*

Or perhaps Elijah experienced a sudden puncture in his spiritual tire and thought, *Oh, no! I just can't take anymore, God. Won't the pressure ever stop? Doesn't this life with You ever get any easier? Can't I just lie back and coast for a while?*

We don't know Elijah's exact thoughts just then, but we can trace his downward spiritual spiral. He tumbles from a magnificent mountaintop experience into fear, depression, doubts about God and himself, discouragement, disillusionment and despair. Elijah even began thinking thoughts of self-destruction. He was down and out for the count

Elijah ran as far as Beersheba and left his servant there,

then continued to stumble into the desert another day's journey. Finally, he could go no further. He collapsed under a juniper tree and begged God to take his life (1 Kings 19:4). He was saying, "I've had enough, Lord, take me home! Nothing in life excites me any longer. I have nothing to live for, no goals to reach, nothing that I can really get excited about doing anymore. Why don't You just let me die?"

Of course, Elijah wasn't serious about dying. If he had been, all he needed to do was wait until Jezebel found him. But Elijah *felt* like dying, and sometimes that seems just as bad.

The lights were on in Elijah's eyes, but nobody was home. The fire was flickering, fading . . . almost ready to go out . . . but Elijah's God loved him too much to allow that to happen.

15

Coming Back From the Point of No Return

Many times, the priorities in your life must be re-ordered to allow time for rest and relaxation. You needn't feel guilty about that.

Less than a mile beyond the tranquil waters that flow quietly beneath the Grand Island Bridge toward Niagara Falls is an infamous place that every boater fears: "The Point of No Return." Once a boat has gone beyond this point, the power of the current increases exponentially, sweeping everything in its path along to an inevitable, horrifying, pounding slam-dunk onto the rugged rocks one hundred sixty feet below. Only a miracle can save a person once he or she has passed the point of no return.

Elijah was heading to the point of no return. And perhaps you are, too. As you think about Elijah being tossed about by that seething, pitching current, you may want to examine your own life. You may find that you and this Bible hero have a lot in common.

How did Elijah—a man of fabulous faith against incredible odds, a man who had known stupefying spiritual successes that you and I hardly dare dream about—become so disillusioned that he felt like dying? Let's check it out.

That Oh, So Lonesome Feeling

1. Elijah was exhausted.

Physically, mentally, emotionally and spiritually, the man was wiped out. And it's important to note that he became exhausted right in the middle of doing God's work.

"Wait a minute," you may be saying. "Didn't you mention earlier that God's power was sufficient so we could run and not get tired, walk and not grow weary? (Isaiah 40:31) How could God's man become exhausted while doing God's work?"

In Elijah's case, Scripture doesn't say for sure, but we can make some intelligent guesses from what it does say. Maybe Elijah was getting just a bit cocky at this point, or perhaps he was beginning to rely on his own energies rather than God's supernatural provisions. Maybe he simply ran ahead of the Lord. He certainly hadn't taken any time to wait upon the Lord, the one condition upon which the promise of Isaiah 40:31 rests.

2. Elijah may have been naive about the devil's tactics and power.

Maybe he honestly thought that by defeating the 850 Satanic prophets he had destroyed the threat to Israel and to himself once and for all. Elijah learned the hard way that Satan does not give up easily. Even after absorbing a devastating defeat, such as the loss of 850 of his representatives, the devil will counterattack again and again.

A group of people were praising the Lord one Sunday morning because a leading adult bookstore in the area, one which they had prayed and picketed against, mysteriously burned to the ground. The Christians considered the fire an answer to prayer, as it may well have been. Their blazing faith and enthusiasm were severely quenched a few days later, however, when the owners erected a brand new building almost overnight. In a few weeks, the pornography business was bigger and "better" than ever.

Elijah may have assumed that because he had scored such a rousing victory, significantly decimating the devil's ranks, the enemy was simply going to roll over and give up. It didn't happen. Jezebel jeered, "Elijah, you mess with me, boy, and I'm going to mess right back!"

Elijah wasn't expecting Jezebel's response, and that's about all it took to snap his streak of confidence. He took off for the wilderness, hoping to hide in the desert.

There's something to be learned from Elijah's experience. As you work for the Lord, be extremely careful to operate under the fresh anointing of His Holy Spirit, using His power and His direction to guide you. Otherwise, the devil will simply wear you down. Your strength will become depleted; your resources will run low; your patience will wear thin. And then the least little disturbance will defeat you. You may find yourself giving in to temptations that you would ordinarily reject. Remember, it is not by your strength or might that the job will be done, but by the power of the Holy Spirit (Zechariah 4:6).

3. Perhaps Elijah had developed a perfectionist complex.

When he dejectedly cried out to God to take his life, he slips in a line almost as an aside: "O LORD, take my life, for I am not better than my fathers" (1 Kings 19:4).

What was he saying? "Aw, my ancestors messed up with God and I guess I did, too. They weren't able to defeat the demonic influences in their day, and neither have I."

Sound familiar?

An alcoholic told me, "My dad was a drunk and before that, his dad was a drunk. I guess I'll just be a drunk, too.

It runs in my family."

I've heard young people say, "I'm just a *C* student. I always get *C*'s. Always have, always will. Dad says that when he was in school, he got nuthin' but *C*'s too."

Elijah was feeling, "I'll never be good enough. I guess I just don't measure up."

But wait a minute! Who said he had to measure up? And according to whose standards? The Lord had called Elijah to do what *Elijah* was to do, not what He had called anyone else to do.

Multitudes in the body of Christ suffer from a similar sort of inadequacy syndrome:

"I'm not witnessing to as many people as Joe is."

"I don't have the same spiritual gift that Sally has."

"I can't sing like he can."

"I wish I could play an instrument the way she does."

Understand that God has not called you to meet anyone else's expectations or to compare yourself with anyone's successes or failures. He has called you to be faithful and obedient to His instructions for *your* life.

Elijah had a desire to do better than his predecessors, which seemed highly noble. But watch out! You can run yourself ragged attempting to fulfill somebody else's image of what *you* are supposed to be. Be what God wants you to be, nothing more and certainly nothing less.

4. Elijah's perfectionism led to isolationism.

On Mount Carmel, Elijah lamented, "I alone am left a prophet of the LORD" (1 Kings 18:22).

As you read the scriptural account, you want to say, "Hold on there, Elijah! Not *all* the people of Israel were following the devil's crowd. Not everyone clamored after Ahab and Jezebel. What about your buddy, Obadiah? What about the one hundred prophets Obadiah has hidden in a cave? Okay, so they aren't the most courageous men of God, but they are still part of the team! And Elijah, don't forget about your own servant. He's been with you through thick and thin."

Later, God revealed to Elijah that *seven thousand* prophets had not bowed down to Baal. But Elijah had been too busy, too caught up in his own ministry, to notice the existence of other men of God.

I once heard a famous evangelist say to his audience, "Nobody else is telling you the truth, but I am." At the time, I thought, *Watch out, Brother. You're setting yourself up for a fall.* Although greatly saddened, I was hardly surprised when a few months later I learned of his spiritual demise.

It is always dangerous to think that you have a corner on understanding the way God works. When you get so preoccupied with what you are doing for God that you fail to see what God is doing in the rest of the world, beware! When you are not aware of, or refuse to acknowledge, what God is doing in and through other parts of the body, you become isolated, a spiritual Lone Ranger.

If you isolate yourself from people, there will be nobody there to help you when you have a problem or a need. When Elijah became discouraged and disillusioned, his view was limited to, "I alone am left; and they seek my life, to take it away" (1 Kings 19:14). In fear and wounded pride, Elijah had even abandoned his faithful servant. Now there was no one to share his load, no one to help bear his grief, no one to whom he could unburden his heart.

One of the best bits of advice I have ever received came from a good friend of mine. With hands on her hips, feet squared and jaw set, she approached me like John Wayne. With one shot, she blew me out of my perfectionistic, isolationist saddle. She said, "Abraham, why don't you just let people know you are human?"

"What?" I cried, taken back by her bluntness. "What are you talking about?"

She blasted me again, "Why don't you let people know you don't always have it together? That you don't have all the answers, that you have doubts and fears, and that sometimes you hurt just like the rest of us—maybe worse!"

I'll always be grateful to a friend who loves me enough to tell me the truth. She wasn't trying to hurt me; she wanted to help me. And she did.

After all, nobody wants to be around someone who thinks he or she is perfect—at least not for long. And if you are trying to convince yourself of your own perfection, you can't allow many people to get close to you. Deep inside you know you are *not* perfect, and if people get close enough to you, they will discover your imperfections. You can't take that risk.

A major cause of spiritual disillusionment is isolation, which is often expressed as a spirit of independence. God never intended for you to function as a Lone Ranger. He intended for you to live within the context of a family, the family of God. If you insist upon isolating yourself, you will become spiritually warped.

We *need* Christians around us who can say, "Yes, I know how that feels. I've been through that."

We *need* mature men and women who cannot only say, "This is the way; walk in it," but who will also honestly admit, "I've been down that path, and you can take my word for it—it's a dead end."

We *need* brothers and sisters who will say, "I understand how you are hurting."

We *need* people to whom we can be accountable, people who love us enough to look us in the eyes and tell us the truth. Elijah isolated himself from his friends and spiritual fellowship, and it almost killed him.

5. Elijah felt that he had no future.

That is a depressing place to be. When Jezebel threatened him, he forgot that his future was in God's hands, not hers. When the times got tough, he got going all right, but in the wrong direction! Elijah said, "Aw, what's the use? I might as well give up. I'm tired. It's all over. The glory days are gone forever. Why try anymore? What is there to hope for?"

Tragically, Elijah had lost his vision. He had lost sight of what God had called him to do with his life. Worse still, he had lost his vision of God Himself! Subsequently, when he no longer had a correct perception of God, he no longer had any self-esteem either. Without God, human beings become meaningless, cosmic accidents, devoid of any intrinsic value. No purpose, no plan, no future.

Turning Your Depression Into Power

What can God do with a guy in Elijah's state of mind? Frankly, not much. What can God do *about* a person like that? Quite a lot, if the person is willing to let God work. There were five areas of need in Elijah's life, and the Lord provided five answers to his problems. Let's look at them.

1. Elijah laid down and slept.

Sometimes the most spiritual thing you can do is get some rest. Honest! God will not berate you for lying down on the job. He knows the need even better than you do.

Elijah was physically depleted. Can you imagine the amount of energy he expended in the challenge between he and the prophets of Baal on Mount Carmel? Then he sprinted to Jezreel. No wonder he was tired!

At that point, Elijah did not need another sermon, song or Bible study. He needed *sleep.*

God is much more practical than we are. He prefers

to meet the immediate need first.

As my psychologist friend Kevin Leman often says, "When little Buford spills his milk on the floor, we don't need a sermon. We don't need a lecture. We need a rag!"

Many times, the priorities in your life must be re-ordered to allow time for rest, relaxation, exercise, vacations and time away with friends or family. You needn't feel guilty about that.

I was raised in a church environment in which it was considered "more spiritual" to "burn out for God." One of our favorite hymns was, "Let Me Burn Out For Thee." Many in our congregation interpreted the lyrics literally, though I'm certain that was not the intent of the hymn writer.

When we are down and out, we tend to believe that if we can only increase our efforts a bit, we can pull out of the nose-dive. We work longer hours and burn more midnight oil, and before we know it, we're running on fumes!

When I was pastoring, one of the greatest gifts I had was a group of elders who had enough sanctified common sense to say, "Ken, you look tired. Go home and get some rest."

Once, when I was apologizing for missing a fellowship meeting, I told one of my co-workers, "I'm real sorry that I won't be able to attend. I've been away quite a bit lately, and I just need to spend the evening at home with my family."

The man looked back at me and said, "I'd be disappointed in you if you did otherwise. That's the best example you could set for us." Most pastors would give their right arm for board members like that.

2. God had Elijah get something to eat.

I'm amazed at how people "over-spiritualize" this part of Elijah's story. I've heard some say that Elijah's need was for spiritual food, the Word of God. Others talk of Jesus, the bread of life, being the satisfaction of Elijah's famished soul.

All of these things may be true. They just don't happen to be what the Scripture says! The Word says that Elijah ate some bread, drank some water and then laid down again (1 Kings 19:6).

Has it ever occurred to you that one of the reasons you are not as spiritually effective as you desire might be directly attributable to an atrocious physical diet?

Think of the awful things people put into their bodies nowadays! Foods high in sugar and low in nutrition, junk foods, fatty foods, salty foods, fried foods . . . Oh boy, I've gone to meddlin' now!

And can you believe the huge number of people who still insist on smoking cigarettes and cigars? What? Do you need a personal message telling you that there's a fire on one end and a fool on the other?

The tobacco companies are already required by law to print ominous warnings on their products and advertisements. That should be enough to scare the smoke out of any semi-conscious human being.

Your body is a temple of the Holy Spirit. You may need to start taking better care of God's property! The apostle Paul writes:

> Do you not know that your body is a temple of the Holy Spirit who is in you, whom you have from God, and that you are not your own? For you have been bought with a price: therefore glorify God in your body (1 Corinthians 6:19,20).

Elijah rested. He ate and drank and rested some more. Then he arose and walked all the way to Horeb, a forty-day journey.

3. The Lord allowed Elijah to get in touch with his feelings.

As I said previously, there is nothing wrong with telling God your side of the story. It may seem a bit redundant, since He knows already, but it's usually good therapy.

Elijah was holed up in a cave when the word of the Lord came to him. It was a gentle word, without accusation or condemnation. Mildly chastising, God asked, "What are you doing here, Elijah?"

Whew! Has God ever asked you that question? It really makes you squirm, doesn't it? "Why are you so down? Why such a long face? How long are you going to hide?" All of those questions and more were rolled into that one simple query, "What are you doing here, Elijah?"

Elijah immediately had a reply, a response that he probably had been rehearsing for almost a month and a half now:

> I have been very zealous for the LORD, the God of hosts; for the sons of Israel have forsaken Thy covenant, torn down Thine altars and killed Thy prophets with the sword. And I alone am left; and they seek my life, to take it away (1 Kings 19:10).

Elijah was blurting out his true feelings. And what Elijah did not say but probably thought was, *Nothing has changed! After all of my efforts, laying my life on the line, stepping out in faith and even seeing You perform miracles, basically everything remains status quo. The people who are supposed to be spiritual leaders are worshipping gods they have made themselves. And Your people have left me to stand all by myself. It's You and me against the world, Lord, and I'm just getting a little tired of it. You wanted to know why I'm here? That's why I'm here!*

4. God gave Elijah a fresh vision of His majesty and power.

Elijah was disillusioned with God, with other believers and with himself. Nevertheless, the Lord did not pamper His man. He directed him outside the cave where God put on a spectacular sound and light show. Scripture records:

> And a great and strong wind was rending the mountains and breaking in pieces the rocks before the LORD; but the LORD was not in the wind. And after the wind an earthquake, but the LORD was not in the earthquake. And after the earthquake a fire, but the LORD was not in the fire; and after the fire a sound of a gentle blowing (1 Kings 19:11,12).

God was showing Elijah His sheer power, but He didn't stop there. He also sent the soft, gentle wind, perhaps a symbol of His Holy Spirit. It was almost as if He were saying, "Elijah, if I wished, I could blast you into oblivion. But I desire to come to you in the sweetness of My Spirit, in soothing, healing grace and love. I, the God of awesome power, am interested in you." God did not debate with Elijah; He merely reminded him who He is.

In his book *Spiritual Burnout,* Malcolm Smith comments:

> We come to God and demand a formula, a series of steps we can tell others we followed to get out of the pit of spiritual exhaustion. But God frustrates us, He doesn't give us a formula ... He gives us Himself! Understand who He is, and everything begins to fall into place. The answer to spiritual burnout is to respond to God afresh, and discover a new relationship with Him.[1]

5. God gave Elijah a fresh assignment.

After the powerful display of His presence, God asked Elijah a second time, "What are you doing here, Elijah?" You would think that having witnessed the staggering revelation of God, Elijah might have come up with an appropriate answer. Instead, he repeated his "woe is me" story. We can only guess what God might have done had Elijah responded more positively. Nevertheless, God did not cast him off. God gave Elijah a new job, part of which involved the selection and training of his successor, Elisha.

If after you receive a fresh revelation of God, you choose to continue in the doldrums of disillusionment and despair, the Lord will allow you to do so! He has not created you as a robot. He will not force you to trust Him. If you refuse to believe the Lord for His best, He will not argue with you. He will simply find someone else who will!

Yet, even in the selection of Elisha, there was a promise to Elijah. God was showing him that He still had plans for Elijah and the people of Israel. He had not written them off. They would have a glorious future.

God may be saying something similar to you. He may be saying, "You don't need a formula. You need a fresh revelation of Me. The reason you are still here is that I am not finished with you. Therefore, *you* are not yet finished!"

Sense the earth shake as He allows you to stand on holy ground. Listen to the voice of His Spirit in the gentle, blowing wind. And feel the warmth of a rekindled love.

16

From Disillusioned to Dis-Illusioned

Four simple, practical principles that will help you expose the illusions that the devil is using to destroy your faith.

The world desperately needs more disillusioned Christians. The church lacks vision and power because we have so few disillusioned Christians. *Disillusioned*, that is, in the truest sense of the word. Confused? Let me explain.

The dictionary defines an illusion as "the state or fact of being intellectually deceived or misled; a misleading image presented to the vision; perception of something objectively existing in such a way as to cause misinterpretation of its actual nature." Considering the potential dangers of illusions, the great devotional writer Oswald Chambers implores that we be *dis-illusioned* Christians.

Rather than using the commonly held meaning of disillusionment, Chambers defines *dis-illusion* as being devoid of false illusions. We need to be stripped of misleading images and divested of all pretense. In *The Discipline of Disillusionment*, Chambers writes:

> *Dis-illusionment* means that there are no more false judgments in life. . . . disillusionment may leave us

cynical and unkindly severe in our judgment of others, but the *dis-illusionment* which comes from God brings us to the place where we see men and women as they really are, and yet there is no cynicism, we have no stinging, bitter things to say. Many of the cruel things in life spring from the fact that we suffer from illusions. We are not true to one another as *facts*; we are only true to our ideas of one another. Everything is either delightful and fine, or mean and dastardly, according to our ideal.[1]

Although many of Chambers' writings lean toward being deep and mystical, the man was a realist and, when rightly understood, his spiritual insights are eminently practical. He constantly urged others to get their heads out of the clouds and live by faith in the fact of God's Word, not in the fantasy world of illusions.

Throughout this book I have attempted to give usable tips to help you overcome or avoid spiritual disillusionment. Now I want to offer four simple, practical principles that will help you become a *dis-illusioned* Christian, a believer who has exposed the illusions that the devil is using to deceive you and destroy your faith.

1. Get Into the Word

One of the reasons the devil succeeds in deceiving devout Christians is our lack of spiritual strength and understanding. Just as you need physical food to survive and function properly, you need spiritual food as well. Reading books about the Bible is noble, but ingesting God's Word itself is the only way to guarantee proper nourishment.

Nowadays, we have a plethora of translations and paraphrases to help us understand the Scriptures. We also have Bibles on cassette tapes, Bibles on computer disks, Bibles in Braille, large-print Bibles, small-print Bibles. If you sincerely desire to study God's Word, you can find a Bible that is suitable for you.

Prayer is an important companion to your regular intake of God's Word. Develop the habit of praying daily. Again, do whatever works for you, but do it! Some people enjoy getting up an hour early every day to spend some time reading the Bible and praying. Others prefer to close their day in this manner. Fine. The important part is that you spend time in the presence of God.

If you have been neglecting the spiritual disciplines of Bible reading and prayer, I strongly urge you to re-institute them in your life. But beware of becoming legalistic. There are no established daily minimum requirements. Just do what brings life and energy to your spirit.

Recently, I was rummaging through some old files and I ran across a spiritual regimen I had imposed upon myself right after graduation from college. As I looked down the list, I thought, *Wow! How naive I was!* These were my goals for each day:

- Review five words in an English dictionary.

- Review five words in a Greek dictionary.

- Read five entries in an encyclopedia.

- Translate two to five verses of Scripture from Greek to English.

- Memorize one verse of Scripture.

- Read twenty chapters of the Bible: five in the New Testament, five in the Old Testament, five from Psalms and five from Proverbs.

- One hour minimum for research and study.

- One hour minimum for prayer and spiritual meditation.

No wonder I became disillusioned! To do all of that on a daily basis would be a full-time job. Fortunately, I soon realized I had set my goals too high so I adjusted them . . . downward. Don't allow your devotional time to become regulated by unrealistic goals. You'll only get discouraged.

Make time in your schedule for a quiet, unhurried, devotional time with God on a regular basis. I have never met a disillusioned Christian who has an exciting, vibrant, devotional life with God. But I have met many Christians who have allowed that time to be replaced by a "higher priority," only to see their spiritual energy dissipate.

2. Deal Drastically With Willful Disobedience

Someone has said, "Keep short accounts with God," and that makes sense to me. In order to do so, you must deal drastically with any deliberate disobedience to the will of God for your life. Do not coddle, nurture or tolerate known sin in any way. Confess it, repent of it and ask God to give you the power to overcome it in the future. Sin in the life of a believer is every bit as destructive as sin in the life of an unbeliever. Sin blocks the flow of God's power in our lives.

A young pastor came in my office to see me. "I just don't sense God's presence anymore," he confided. "When I read the Bible it seems dry and lifeless. When I pray I feel as though God is a million miles away. I don't have any joy or power in preaching. I have lost my love for the people, and my congregation is about ready to ask me to leave. What's wrong with me?"

We talked for a while about disillusionment and disappointments in the ministry, about his personal study habits and devotional life. Then I asked him matter-of-factly, "Is there any known, willful sin in your life?"

The question caught him off guard and he answered before thinking, "Yes, there is."

"What is it?" I pressed.

"Well, you know that our church doesn't have much money, and my wife and I receive a pretty meager salary. So last year, when I was doing our income tax return, I fudged on the figures a little. Nothing major. I just increased our housing deduction enough to receive a refund from the government. But it's been bothering me ever since."

"What are you going to do about it?" I asked.

"What *can* I do?" he returned. "We've already spent the money, and if I tell the Internal Revenue Service now, they will put me in jail. How would that look in the papers: 'Local Minister Goes to Jail!' I can't afford that."

"Can you afford to lose everything else?" I asked straightforwardly.

His mouth gaped open. "Do you think it is *that* serious?"

"Well, I don't know, but it sure seems to be. Obviously, your sin is enough to separate you from God's presence."

We talked further and then knelt down by the sofa and prayed together. He confessed his sin concerning the income tax refund and received forgiveness from God. I was about to stand to my feet, when I felt him tugging at my sleeve.

"Wait," he said fervently, "there's more!"

I knelt down beside him again and listened as the young preacher opened up his heart and, like a flood tide of dirty, dammed-up water, poured out his confession to God. When we finally stood to our feet, about a half an hour later, I knew that God had heard and answered his prayer. The young man's countenance radiated with a brightness that only comes from a clean heart.

A month later, I saw him at a minister's conference. He could hardly wait to tell me his story.

"I was scared to death, but I knew I had to do it," he

began. "I called the I.R.S. and confessed what I had done. They suggested that I gather up my receipts and come in to talk about it, which I did. The agent figured out the amount of tax due, plus a penalty and allowed me to pay the bill right there, with no further repercussions or investigations!"

"Great!" I replied. "How are things going at the church?"

"You won't believe it," he gushed. "I knew that I was forgiven by God and by the government, but I felt I owed my congregation an explanation. During a regular morning worship service, I stood up before I was to preach and confessed what I had done. When I finished speaking, several men in the congregation made their way to the front of the church and asked if we would pray for them. They had cheated on their taxes, too! Others stepped out of the crowd and began confessing their shortcomings and sins. It was a time of genuine revival."

"What about your personal life?" I probed.

"I'm doing fantastic! The Scriptures have come alive again, and when I pray, I know God is there. I've been preaching with a power and a freedom that I have never known before. And guess what . . . the church has given us a raise in salary!"

Not every confession and restitution works out so neatly. Nevertheless, don't allow sin to do its dirty work. If you have been tolerating willful disobedience to God in your life, confess, repent and find a fresh freedom through forgiveness. Don't live under the illusion that one little sin won't matter. Become a *dis*-illusioned Christian.

3. Establish a Sabbath

Many Christians fail to take the Sabbath seriously, and I believe we do so at our own peril. God did not create us to be perpetual motion machines. He has set aside special times for His people to come together, to praise and worship Him, and to rest and be refreshed themselves.

When God gave the Ten Commandments to Moses, He specifically included clear instructions regarding the Sabbath. He said:

> Remember the sabbath day, to keep it holy. Six days you shall labor and do all your work, but the seventh day is a sabbath of the LORD your God; in it you shall not do any work, you or your son or your daughter, your male or your female servant or your cattle or your sojourner who stays with you. For in six days the LORD made the heavens and the earth, the sea and all that is in them, and rested on the seventh day; therefore the LORD blessed the sabbath day and made it holy (Exodus 20:8-11).

This command was repeated and expanded throughout the Old Testament. By the time of Jesus, the legalistic Pharisees had devised an entire system of outlandish Sabbath-keeping laws. Jesus, however, bucked their system by healing (Matthew 12:8-12), picking grain to eat (Mark 2:23) and doing good on the Sabbath (Matthew 12:12). He never rescinded the original commandment concerning the Sabbath; He merely reminded His disciples and His critics that "the Sabbath was made for man, and not man for the Sabbath. Consequently, the Son of Man is Lord even of the Sabbath" (Mark 2:27,28).

In the Old Testament, Sabbath breaking was considered a capital crime, punishable by death (Exodus 35:2). In the New Testament, there is no such condemnation. This frees modern believers in many ways. But a type of death sentence may still exist for those who neglect to take at least one day per week for rest, reflection, refreshment and redirection. The modern-day equivalent of the death sentence may well be spiritual disillusionment, exhaustion and burnout

Something restorative happens when you are able to take one day out of seven and set it apart as a Sabbath.

Brent is a vice president of a Fortune-500 company. Many other junior executives with his company are workaholics. They work seven days a week, nearly every week. Brent, however, refuses to do so. He takes Saturday as his day off and Sunday as a Sabbath.

"Each Friday afternoon, as I am getting ready to leave, the company is teetering on the brink of collapse," Brent told me. "People are running around, trying to push through some last-minute deals. Phones are buzzing, and everyone has that look of exhaustion on their faces. As I pack up my briefcase and head for the door, somebody usually tries to make me feel guilty for not working the weekend. In the early days, I did feel guilty that they were working and I wasn't. Not anymore. Now I feel pity for them. They aren't forced to work. They want the overtime pay.

"Once I'm out of the office and home with my family, I try to forget all about my career. Saturday is our play day and often a time to get the odd jobs done around the house. But Sunday is our Sabbath. We go to church, read, relax and rest. When I go back to work on Monday, I find that the company has not collapsed, and that there are just as many phones ringing and people screaming at each other. The only difference is that I am physically, mentally and spiritually rejuvenated and many of my colleagues are even more frazzled. I'm a better person the other six days of the week because of that one day designated as a Sabbath."

When and how should you keep the Sabbath? The New Testament does not say exactly. Personally, my family regards Sunday as our Sabbath, although I have sincere Christian friends who choose to set aside Saturday as their Sabbath. And I know pastors who work so hard on Sunday that they need to take another day out of the week as their Sabbath.

We refuse to become legalistic about Sabbath-keeping. In our family we've set some guidelines that allow for a great deal of latitude while still preserving the specialness of the Sabbath. If possible, we refrain from buying or selling on the Sabbath. We also avoid working, especially if the job could be done any other day of the week. As a general guide for what we should or shouldn't do, we ask questions like: "Is the activity relaxing, restful or restorative? Does this thing draw us closer to the Lord or push us further away from Him? Will we be better or worse the rest of the week for having engaged in this activity on the Sabbath?"

The answers to these questions are extremely subjective and will vary according to the individual answering them. What is relaxing for one person may be work for another. A round of golf may be a relaxing, restorative activity for someone on the Sabbath. For me, playing golf would be much closer to work, especially the way I play!

However you choose to observe the Sabbath, I encourage you to do so. By setting apart one day for the Lord, it is a reminder of His reign in your life. It is also one of the surest ways to keep your problems and opportunities in proper perspective. It will help you avoid spiritual burnout and disillusionment, while dispelling the illusion that you're Super Christian!

Remember the Sabbath and keep it holy.

The fourth principle to help you overcome spiritual disillusionment is so important that it merits a chapter of its own. We'll take a look at that next.

17

Keep Your Eyes
on Jesus

*Jesus says simply: "You follow Me!" That's it.
Nothing more. Nothing less. Nothing else.*

My dentist has a strange sense of humor. He informed me that I had a cavity that must be drilled and filled. Then he asked, "What kind of filling would you prefer? Gold? Silver amalgam? Or chocolate?" Smart aleck.

We prefer life to be sweet and easy. We want things to work out nicely, painlessly and fairly. Unfortunately, that sort of life is an illusion.

My friend Joel Freeman wrote a book titled *"God Is Not Fair"* (Here's Life Publishers). When I first read the title, I thought, *Joel, Joel! You've lost your senses, son! Of course, God is fair. Why after all, He's . . . He's . . . well, He's God! He's got to be fair!*

"No, He doesn't," says Joel. Not if by "fair" you mean that God treats us all the same way. We want Him to be that way, but He is not.

We expect our Christian lives to be lived with the same amount of pain, suffering, joy and laughter as everyone else. But life just does not work that way. Although God's character remains the same and His love for each of us remains a constant, He works differently in each of our individual lives. That's hard to accept sometimes, especially for dedicated disciples of Jesus.

But, Lord . . .

After His resurrection, Jesus reinforced this principle for Peter. Jesus informed Peter that his life was not going to be chocolate-covered or sugar-coated. He said:

> "Truly, truly, I say to you, when you were younger, you used to gird yourself, and walk wherever you wished; but when you grow old, you will stretch out your hands, and someone else will gird you, and bring you where you do not wish to go." Now this He said, signifying by what kind of death he would glorify God. And when He had spoken this, He said to him, "Follow Me!" (John 21:18,19)

Jesus was calling Peter to an absolute, irrevocable commitment to follow Him, no matter what. He says the same to you and me. Peter responds to the Lord's command in a way most of us can identify with:

> Peter, turning around, saw the disciple whom Jesus loved following them. . . . Peter therefore seeing him said to Jesus, "Lord, and what about this man?" (John 21:20,21)

Isn't that so like us? We immediately become obsessed with what God is doing, or not doing, in the life of somebody else. We are constantly concerned about comparing and contrasting our lives with others. Of course, people often protest, "Hey, I'm not judging anyone; I'm just a fruit inspector."

Yeah, right.

"God, I know what You are requiring of me, but what about that other person?" We often attempt to take the pressure off ourselves by focusing attention negatively on someone else.

Perhaps that is what Peter was doing. "Okay, Lord, I've got it. You want me to follow You no matter what. Right. No problem. But what about this guy? What about dear, little Johnny, Your beloved?"

Peter's response is classic. He wasn't necessarily expressing a lack of love for John, although he was not exactly praying for him either. And I don't believe Peter was jealous of the younger disciple who apparently was going to live longer than himself (which he did).

Peter's response was simply a typical remark emanating from a carnal, unsanctified curiosity: "Lord, what about John? What are You going to do with him? You're telling me that one of these days I am going to have to give up my life for You, but what about my buddy over there? Aren't You going to give *him* something tough to do, too? Do I have to carry this load alone? Come on, Lord! It doesn't seem fair!"

Isn't it amazing how easy it is to develop an inordinate, and often inappropriate, interest in the will of God for somebody else's life?

"You Follow Me!"

But Jesus would not allow Peter to shift the focus away from himself. Jesus brought the spotlight right back on Peter with a gentle, yet emphatic, rebuke:

> Jesus said to him, "If I want him to remain until I come, what is that to you? You follow Me!" (John 21:22)

Whap! In a nice but no-nonsense sort of way, Jesus was belting Peter right in the teeth. He was saying, "Peter, mind your own business. I'll take care of John. You take care of what I have given you to do. Must I remind you of where you have come from? Must I mention again your sin, your failures, your recent denials of Me? No. Peter, you just take care of *you*, and that will keep you quite busy."

The Lord's words must have seared into Peter's heart, and no doubt, that is what Jesus intended for them to do. He was putting the pressure on Peter right at the most sensitive point: the level of his unconditional commitment. Jesus knew that Peter loved Him, but now He was asking for more. He wanted Peter totally available and fully committed, with no strings attached. Jesus was calling His man to stand alone with Him, whether or not he had help and support from friends, family or colleagues.

Jesus' command to Peter was perfectly calculated to get the fisherman off the shore and onto the hook! Or you could say, He wanted Peter out of the fish-frying pan and into the fire.

Yes, as Christians, we are family, and in a real sense, what strikes your life affects mine, whether it be positive or negative. At the same time, though, God is at work in our individual lives, and He may be working in your life in a different manner than He does mine. Every time I try to figure out what God is doing in another person's life, Jesus says, "Hey, Ken. What is that to you? You follow Me!"

The Choice Is Ours

You may be disillusioned. You may be experiencing terribly difficult days. Perhaps God is putting the pressure on your most sensitive spot. He may be bringing you through a desperately demanding period in your life or through a dry, dusty wilderness. Possibly you have been humiliated as you have struggled to hold onto your faith in an entirely new or unfamiliar set of circumstances.

I said at the outset that I have no easy answers for you. All I can tell you is to keep your eyes on Jesus! You've probably been tempted to stick your head up, gawk around and say, "Lord, what about him (or her)? God, this is not fair! You know I love you. Now, what's all this about?"

Or perhaps you have been tempted to look across the aisle at church, or across the street from where you live, or maybe even across your dining room table, and think, *Lord, why aren't You dealing with that person the way You are turning the heat up on me? Why do they have it so cozy and comfortable?*

If you listen carefully, you will probably hear the Spirit of Jesus say, "What is that to you? You follow Me!"

Understand, God is not calling everyone to do what He has called you to do. He is not asking everyone to endure what He has allowed you to endure. He is working in each one of our lives in wonderfully different ways, so each of us can magnify and glorify the name of Jesus.

That's why you and I have no right to feel sorry for ourselves when He is taking us through the tough times, the lonely times, the disillusioning times. Similarly, we have no right to be smug, arrogant or self-righteous when God is blessing the socks right off our feet! He says simply: "You follow Me!" That's it. Nothing more. Nothing less.

Nothing else.

Horatio Spafford was a man who understood this truth well. Spafford was a successful Chicago lawyer, a friend of such inspiring spiritual giants as D. L. Moody, Ira Sankey and Phillip Bliss. In 1873, the family doctor recommended a vacation for Horatio's wife, so the couple planned a trip to Europe by ship.

Right before their departure, a matter arose that delayed Mr. Spafford's trip. Rather than ruining the vacation for his family, Spafford sent his wife and four lovely daughters on ahead, promising he would join them in just a few days. Mrs. Spafford and the girls set sail for Europe without him.

On November 22, in a tragic accident, the ship on

which the women were sailing was rammed by an English vessel. The Spafford's ship sank in less than thirty minutes. With the roaring waves of the Atlantic Ocean rolling over them, Mrs. Spafford and the girls were tossed from the ship as though they were tiny porcelain dolls. Mrs. Spafford was miraculously rescued, but all four of the girls drowned in the sea.

On December 1, Mrs. Spafford cabled her husband a stark message: "Saved. Alone."

Horatio Spafford bought passage aboard the first ship he could find that was sailing to England. Out on the high, rolling seas, the ship passed close to the exact spot where the accident a few days before had claimed the lives of his four daughters. With tears pouring down his face as he looked out over the rolling waves where his daughters had died, Horatio Spafford penned these words:

> When peace like a river attendeth my way,
> When sorrows like sea billows roll,
> Whatever my lot, Thou has taught me to say,
> "It is well; it is well with my soul."[1]

Spafford had every reason to be a disillusioned Christian, but he refused to wallow in despair. Instead, he became a dis-illusioned Christian. He kept his eyes on Jesus, and his testimony and music have been a source of blessing to millions.

You have a similar choice to make. Perhaps you have been discouraged or disillusioned by failures in the lives of fellow Christians. Jesus says, "What is that to you? You follow Me!"

Possibly you have been blaming somebody else for keeping you from following Jesus as closely as you know you should. Maybe you feel that your spouse, your parents, your church, your spiritual leaders or perhaps even God Himself has let you down.

Jesus says, "You follow Me!"

Today, it is time to move from being the disillusioned Christian to a *dis*-illusioned Christian, one who has radically committed your life to Jesus Christ, come what may. Do it! Do it *now*.

Notes

Chapter 1

1. Charles R. Swindoll, *Growing Strong in the Seasons of Life* (Portland, OR: Multnomah Press, 1983), pp. 25-26.

Chapter 2

1. Jim Conway, *Men In Mid-Life Crisis* (Elgin, IL: David C. Cook Publishing Co., 1978), pp. 11-12.
2. Hannah Whitall Smith, *The Christian's Secret of a Happy Life* (Old Tappan, NJ: Fleming H. Revell, 1942), p. 13.

Chapter 3

1. Gordon MacDonald, *Renewing Your Spiritual Passion* (Nashville, TN: Oliver Nelson Books, 1989), p. 47.
2. Barbara Mandrell with George Vecsey, *Get to the Heart* (New York: Bantam Books, 1990), p. 263.
3. Harold Begbie, *The Life of General William Booth* (New York: MacMillen, 1920), p. 422.

Chapter 4

1. Oswald Chambers, *My Utmost For His Highest* (New York: Dodd, Mead and Co., 1954), p. 297.
2. Gail MacDonald, *Keep Climbing* (Wheaton, IL: Tyndale House, 1989), p. 229.
3. David A. Seamands, *Living With Your Dreams* (Wheaton, IL: Victor Books, 1990), pp. 16-17.

Chapter 5

1. Clarence W. Hall, *Samuel Logan Brengle: Portrait of a Prophet* (Chicago, IL: Salvation Army, 1976 edition), p. 89.

Chapter 6

1. David A. Seamands, *Living With Your Dreams* (Wheaton, IL: Victor Books, 1990), p. 86.

Chapter 8

1. Malcolm Smith, *Spiritual Burnout* (Tulsa, OK: Honor Books, 1988), p. 113.

Chapter 9

1. David Wilkerson, *Have You Felt Like Giving Up Lately?* (Old Tappan, NJ: Fleming H. Revell), p. 44.

2. Arthur C. Zepp, *Conscience Alone Not a Safe Guide* (Chicago, IL: The Christian Witness Company, 1913), p. 103.
3. Arthur C. Zepp, *Conscience Alone*, p. 103.
4. C. S. Lewis, *Mere Christianity* (New York: MacMillan Publishing Company, Inc., 1964), p. 172.
5. C. S. Lewis, *Mere Christianity*, p. 174.

Chapter 10
1. Charles R. Swindoll, *The Grace Awakening* (Dallas, TX: Word Publishing, 1990), p. 68.
2. Larry Crabb, *Inside Out* (Colorado Springs: NavPress, 1988), pp. 15-16.

Chapter 11
1. William J. Petersen, *Husbands and Wives* (Wheaton, IL: Tyndale House Publishers, 1989), pp. 174-175.
2. Petersen, *Husbands and Wives*, p. 180.
3. Larry Crabb, *Inside Out* (Colorado Springs, CO: NavPress, 1988), p. 18.

Chapter 13
1. William J. Petersen, *Husbands and Wives* (Wheaton, IL: Tyndale House Publishers, 1989), p. 161.

Chapter 14
1. Helmut Thielicke, *Encounter With Spurgeon* (Grand Rapids: Baker Book House, 1975), p. 214.

Chapter 15
1. Malcolm Smith, *Spiritual Burnout* (Tulsa, OK: Honor Books, 1988), p. 169.

Chapter 16
1. Oswald Chambers, *My Utmost for His Highest* (New York: Dodd, Mead & Company, 1954), pp. 153-154.

Chapter 17
1. Horatio G. Spafford and Phillip Bliss, "It Is Well With My Soul," 1873, P. D.